Cambridge Elements

Elements in Shakespeare Performance
edited by
W. B. Worthen
Barnard College

PERFORMING VISIBLE PREGNANCY IN SHAKESPEARE'S PLAYS

Patricia Lennox
New York University

Shaftesbury Road, Cambridge CB2 8EA, United Kingdom

One Liberty Plaza, 20th Floor, New York, NY 10006, USA

477 Williamstown Road, Port Melbourne, VIC 3207, Australia

314–321, 3rd Floor, Plot 3, Splendor Forum, Jasola District Centre,
New Delhi – 110025, India

103 Penang Road, #05–06/07, Visioncrest Commercial, Singapore 238467

Cambridge University Press is part of Cambridge University Press & Assessment,
a department of the University of Cambridge.

We share the University's mission to contribute to society through the pursuit of
education, learning and research at the highest international levels of excellence.

www.cambridge.org
Information on this title: www.cambridge.org/9781009624459

DOI: 10.1017/9781009624442

© Patricia Lennox 2025

This publication is in copyright. Subject to statutory exception and to the provisions
of relevant collective licensing agreements, no reproduction of any part may take place
without the written permission of Cambridge University Press & Assessment.

When citing this work, please include a reference to the DOI 10.1017/9781009624442

First published 2025

A catalogue record for this publication is available from the British Library

ISBN 978-1-009-62445-9 Paperback
ISSN 2516-0117 (online)
ISSN 2516-0109 (print)

Cambridge University Press & Assessment has no responsibility for the persistence
or accuracy of URLs for external or third-party internet websites referred to in this
publication and does not guarantee that any content on such websites is, or will remain,
accurate or appropriate.

For EU product safety concerns, contact us at Calle de José Abascal, 56, 1°, 28003
Madrid, Spain, or email eugpsr@cambridge.org

Performing Visible Pregnancy in Shakespeare's Plays

Elements in Shakespeare Performance

DOI: 10.1017/9781009624442
First published online: October 2025

Patricia Lennox
New York University

Author for correspondence: Patricia Lennox, pl35@nyu.edu

ABSTRACT: This Element considers pregnant characters and their costumes in the staging of Shakespeare's plays. It examines the connections between a costume and the changing social conventions of pregnancy. It questions mid twentieth-century productions' reduction and elimination of well-established visible pregnancy costumes. It considers the role played by the sexual revolution in the 1960s in visible pregnancy's reinstatement. The Element focusses on the varied significance of its presence to actors and directors and explores the archives to chart this previously under-examined interaction between social conventions, costumes, and the actors who wear them.

KEYWORDS: Shakespeare, performance, costume, pregnancy, gravid body

© Patricia Lennox 2025

ISBNs: 9781009624459 (PB), 9781009624442 (OC)
ISSNs: 2516-0117 (online), 2516-0109 (print)

Contents

	Introduction	1
1	'Big-Bellied' Women: Shakespeare, Pregnancy, and Dressing the Pregnant Character	4
2	The Gravid Body: Juliet, *Measure for Measure*	9
3	Choosing Visibility: Helena, *All's Well That Ends Well*	13
4	Case Study: Hermione, *The Winter's Tale*	18
5	When Pregnancy Is Visible: What Actors Say about Performing Hermione's Pregnancy	53
6	The Pregnant Actress: *The Comedy of Errors* 2021. A Conversation with Phillip Breen and Hedydd Dylan	81
7	Epilogue	85
	References	90

Introduction

1 LADY   Hark ye,
The queen, your mother, rounds apace: we shall
Present our services to a fine new prince
One of these days, and then you'd wanton with us,
If we would have you.
2 LADY   She is spread of late
Into a goodly bulk: good time encounter her!
****

LEONTES   ... let her sport herself
With that she's big with, for 'tis Polixenes
Has made thee swell thus.

The Winter's Tale 2.1,15-20, 60-62[1]

How would a costume showing visible pregnancy be a reflection of social and theatrical practices? That question is explored in this Shakespeare in Performance Element. Shakespeare wrote two plays that require a character to be visibly pregnant during the action on stage. One is a major character, Hermione, queen of Sicilia who gives birth in prison in *The Winter's Tale*, and the other is a minor one, Juliet in *Measure for Measure* who is betrothed to Claudio, pregnant but not yet married. Both women are about to give birth in their early scenes, and both are sent to prison because of their pregnancy. In a third play, *All's Well That Ends Well*, Helena, a major role, announces her pregnancy in the final scene, and some productions have chosen to make it visible, even though there is no indication in the text that the pregnancy is advanced. Each of these plays reflects and manages different issues in costuming and staging pregnancy, including the impact that a realistically sized pregnancy can have on performances. This is part of the way, generally under-acknowledged, that the social politics of women's bodies has on costume practices, and is addressed here specifically through the representations of three pregnant bodies in Shakespeare's plays. The

---

[1] Shakespeare quotations throughout are from the Arden Shakespeare series.

following, designed to be an element in the broader social/sexual/gender discussion, draws upon a range of archival performance-related material, including: prompt books, costume bibles, performance recordings, critical reviews, memoirs, biographies, autobiographies, and artwork. It is also influenced by conversations with theatre practitioners. The goal has been to understand: what the costumes were, how they fitted into the production, how the actors worked with them, and how performing pregnancy with a well-developed gravid body brought the unborn child into the performance. The narrative focuses primarily on twentieth- and twenty-first-century productions, but it starts with Shakespeare's actors.

On Shakespeare's stage his 'great-bellied' pregnant women were played by boy actors in silks and satins (Section 1). This is supported by primary source materials: the information found in theatre manager Philip Henslowe's diaries, actor-manager Edward Alleyn's list of acting apparel and contemporary pregnancy portraits. Taken together, these furnish an image of how well-dressed the pregnant women would have been in the populace and Shakespeare's audiences, and how their reflection was seen in theatre costumes. Moving forward, modern productions' presentation of Juliet's late-term pregnancy in *Measure for Measure* is examined through representative versions demonstrating directors' incorporations of her appearance and costume as an integral part of the play's dark politics of their production (Section 2). With Helena in *All's Well That Ends Well* (Section 3) the director's decision to add or omit a visible pregnancy in her final costume is a late development and a variable part of what has become a popular staging of the play's conclusion as enigmatic. A case study of *The Winter's Tales* (Sections 4 and 5) takes a closer look at Hermione's pregnancy, an important feature in her first two scenes and an influence on her third scene when she is on trial. This is a role usually played by established actresses, some of whom have had a great deal of control over their costumes and have had deep involvement with playing the pregnancy. Important points include Victorian costumes with clearly defined large pregnant bellies, and the minimization and disappearance of any pregnancy in the costumes between 1920 and 1960. The significant effect of the pregnancy prosthesis' return in 1969 is discussed by actresses recalling personal experiences. The wealth of archival material documenting *The Winter's Tale* productions make this a particularly good place to trace the development of the pregnancy costume alongside changing social attitudes. Finally, the story of a recent production's integration of an actor's actual pregnancy into the character of Adrianna, in *The Comedy of Errors*, is discussed with the director and actor (Section 6).

The costumes in the plays discussed here are consistent with the historical pattern for Shakespeare costumes in general: starting with eclecticism, moving through a period of historically 'authentic' (with sets and costumes designed to accord with the play's historical setting); eventually arriving at a time of freely and eclectically choosing, or inventing, place and period for interpretive reasons, though with an understanding of the theatre culture of Shakespeare's own time.[2] The difference is the added complexity of pregnancy. The presence of a visible pregnancy is almost never mentioned in reviews, though for different reasons at different times, so the information often needs to be ferreted out. Research considerations in this study include: costume history, popular fashion, theatrical convention, race, gender, budget, the star system, director choices, design styles, production values, theatre conditions, performance demands, and audience expectations.[3] The study adds to these categories the element of social conventions that censor the female body and govern, both legally and subversively, the social (and theatrical) performance of sexuality, nudity, pregnancy, birth, and motherhood. During much of the twentieth century, pregnancy did not seem suitable in an academic discussion, nor was there a suitably appropriate vocabulary. This eventually disappeared, as seen in Stanley Wells' glowing description in 1987 of Sally Dexter's Hermione: 'high-breasted and ripely pregnant, warm in affection for both her husband and his friend'.[4]

In writing this, further questions emerged that have been applied differently to each of the plays: How has pregnancy been used in the

---

[2] For costume history see de Marly, 1982; Jackson, 2016, 10–20; Hawkins, 2022, 15–23. For historical overview see Potter, 2001, 183–99; Holland, 2001, 199–216; Dobson, 2001, 235–50.

[3] See, for example: Barbrieri, 2017; de Marly, 1982; Escolme, 2020; Hawkins, 2022; Lennox and Mirabella, 2015; MacIntyre, 1992; Monks, 2020; Ribeiro, 2003, and articles in *Studies of Costume and Performance*, vols 1–9, 2016–2024.

[4] Wells, 1987, Shakespeare in Performances in England 1987–8, in Stanley Wells, ed. *Shakespeare Survey 41*. Cambridge: Cambridge University Press. 129–28.

productions? What influenced the pregnancy costume design? What does this tell us about the interrelationship between social conventions and the political construction of pregnancy? Underlying all of this are Carol Chillington Rutter's ground-breaking conversations with actresses in *Clamorous Voices*.[5]

1 'Big-Bellied' Women: Shakespeare, Pregnancy, and Dressing the Pregnant Character

THIRD GENTLEMAN

          Great-bellied women,
That had not half a week to go, like rams
In the old time of war, would shake the press,
And make 'em reel before 'em.

Henry VIII 4.1.78-81

TITANIA

When we have laughed to see the sails conceive
And grow big-bellied with the wonton wind,
Which she with pretty and with swimming gait
Would imitate, and sail upon the land
To fetch me trifles . . ..

A Midsummer Night's Dream 2.1.128-130

Shakespeare wrote in a time that had a robust attitude toward pregnancy. Male writers spoke of being pregnant with their work and of the printer's role as the midwife. The word 'pregnant' was neither taboo, nor indelicate, and the common vernacular referred to pregnant women as 'big-bellied' or 'great bellied'.[6] (When the foetus began to move in the womb it was said to

---

[5] Rutter, 1988.

[6] For Elizabethan and later use of 'big-bellied' see Moncrief, 2007, 30; Hearn, 2020, 11; OED definition and quotes 1592, 1660, 1670. www.oed.com/dictionary/big-bellied.

be 'quick'.[7]) There were well-established rituals attached to the birth, including a prescribed period of time indoors to recover strength, the 'gossips feast', a post-birth gathering of women at the mother's bedside, and 'churching', the religious service that signalled the new mother's re-entry into the community.[8] Hermione, on trial immediately after giving birth, is referring to these when she speaks of her ill treatment: 'The childbed privileges denied which 'longs / To women of all fashion; lastly hurried / Here, to this place, i'th' open air, before / I have got strength of limit' (5.2.102-4). Shakespeare's writing is full of references to pregnancy and birth. These include pregnancies that are variations at any stage from early to late, legalized by marriage or illegitimate. They can be well established, suspected, falsely claimed, dynastic or of little importance. Pregnancies are welcomed, troublesome, and may cause loss and grief. They may expose liaisons and can mean trouble. For the mother they are (sometimes) a source of power but always include pain and a mortal threat. Characters in the plays speak lyrically, as Titania does when remembering her votaress who grew 'big bellied with the wanton wind' but died in childbirth. Pregnancy also creates comic figures, including the undeterred women in *Henry VIII* who have 'not half a week to go' and use their big bellies as battering rams. Pregnancy was the only condition that could spare a woman from hanging, at least until the baby was born, and is falsely claimed by Doll in *Henry IV*, part 2 and Joan la Pucelle in *Henry VI*, part 1.[9]

When these plays were first performed by Shakespeare's acting company, the young male actors playing the women would have been experienced in performing women's roles and moving gracefully in their clothing. They would have been gorgeously dressed in richly coloured and elaborately trimmed costumes. The fabric would have been authentic quality silk, satin, velvet, but its trimmings theatrical substitutions of coloured glass for jewels, thin copper wire replacing fragile lace, fake gold and silver trim, and rabbit fur disguised as ermine. Pieces of clothing would have been acquired

---

[7] In *Love's Labour's Lost* the country woman Jaquenetta is 'quick, the child brags in her belly' 5.2.672

[8] For churching see Jeanne Roberts, 1992, 131.

[9] See, Doll in *Henry IV*, part 2, ed. Bulman, 2016, 414, n. 8–9.

by the playhouse second-hand, and any original embroidery that could not be picked out by the seller would remain as decoration. Hermione's costume would include the shape of a heavily pregnant woman. This is supported by Sara S.B. Thiel's information that between 1603 and 1642, 'the "great belly" becomes part of the ongoing conversation surrounding early modern prosthetics and stage materials [and] many 'pregnancy' plays depict characters whose bellies are visible'.[10]

A plays' costumes were, generally, contemporary clothing, no matter where or when the action was set. Shakespeare's audiences, at court and at the Globe, would have expected Hermione to wear clothing suitable to her station and to be 'big-bellied'. The costume would have been devised by members of the company and, possibly, a tailor (the tyer-man) working with them.[11] Because Elizabethan and Jacobean dress was a combination of separate items that were laced and tied, or pinned together, parts could be used by actors in various combinations to create different costumes. Those for lower-class characters would have been a combination of ordinary clothing (some of it the actors' own clothes), but for characters of higher economic and social brackets theatres used renovated second-hand clothing as the major source for fabrics and trim.

Shakespeare wrote for a structured society where dress was expected to be appropriate to and representative of a person's economic status, social class, gender, affiliations and profession. The same was expected of theatrical performances. Sumptuary Laws were designed to regulate social distinctions in dress by specifying who could wear certain colours, fabrics, furs, and jewels. They applied to actors when offstage, but not when performing. On stage actors were expected to dress as realistically for their character as possible. Clothing was a major item of conspicuous consumption in society and could be very expensive. Its costs were well beyond the purchasing capability of a theatre or acting company, even one as successful as Shakespeare's. Then, as

---

[10] Thiel, Cushion Come Forth: Materializing Pregnancy on the Stuart Stage. For Elizabethan and later use of 'big-bellied' see Moncrief 2007, 30; Hearn, 2020, 11; OED definition and quotes 1592, 1660, 1670. https://www.oed.com/dictionary/big-bellied.

[11] See Jones and Stallybrass, 2000, 176–206; Hawkins, 2022, 15–18.

now, audiences wanted to experience current fashion worn by the wealthy, the powerful, and the royal. To achieve this sense of luxury in productions, theatres bought appropriate second-hand clothing and had a substantial supply available to choose from. Clothing circulated as a currency of exchange: bought, sold, given away, used for payment, stolen, inherited, received as gifts or wages, and purchased as commercial speculation.[12] Additional sources for used costumes came from Jacobean court masques (which did have elaborately designed costumes specific to a production) and civic festivals. Even though items were purchased second-hand, costumes were one of the most expensive items in a theatre's budget. Theatre manager Philip Henslowe's diaries (1593–1608) contain an extensive record of clothing of varying quality and type that had been purchased or held as security for loans, and some of these clothes would end up on stage.[13] Further evidence of the gorgeousness of costumes exists in actor-manager Edward Alleyn's 1598 list of apparel held by his acting company, the Admiral's Men.[14] Typical examples are a crimson robe stripped with gold, faced with ermine, a cloth of gold coat with orange tawny bases, and a doublet of black velvet cut on silver tinsel. Alleyn recorded paying £20 10s 6d, for a 'black velvet cloak with sleeves embroidered all with silver and gold'.[15] Shakespeare's company (the King's Men under James I) would have needed to keep on hand a similar supply of garments for its extensive repertoire and would have spent accordingly.

For the appearance of pregnancy costumes on Shakespeare's stage a third important source of information is available. Between 1560 and 1630 there was a vogue for commissioning portraits of pregnant women to record and celebrate the expected birth, though if the child or mother died they became memorials. Karen Hearn, who identified this sub-genre, includes four illustrations of it in *Picturing Pregnancy*. In the portraits, styles change according to fashion and individual taste, but luxurious dressing remains.

---

[12] See Jones and Stalleybrass, 2000, 17–33. [13] See Foakes, 1961, 2002, 292–93.

[14] Henslowe, 2002, 291–94, see Alleyn's items numbered 1, 3, 4, 9, 15.

[15] Gurr, 2009, 238. He points out that this was more than a third of the cost of Shakespeare's own great house.

Hearn includes pregnancy portraits by Marcus Gheeraerts II (1562–1636) who seemed to make a speciality of them.

In Figure 1, Gheerhaerts' *Portrait of an Unknown Lady* his young woman glows like the pearls that criss-cross her grey dress, sit in her hair, and form her chief jewels. Even the shape of her pregnancy's great roundedness suggests an enormous pearl.[16] The other three portraits depict women, always elaborately and expensively dressed, wearing beautifully decorated layers, including hip or waist length jackets, open and arranged to give prominence to the belly. The clothes and the body's position emphasize their well-developed pregnancy: *Katherine Carey, Lady Knollys* ((1562), artist unknown) is wrapped in layers of black velvet trimmed with white fur and decorated

Figure 1 Celebrating Pregnancy. Marcus Gheerhaerts II, c. 1595, *Portrait of an Unknown Lady*. Photo: Tate.

---

[16] See Engel, 2024, on the iconography of pearls. 'The Paradox of Pearls', 6–27.

with gold accessories; Hans Eworth's *Mildred Cooke, Lady Burghley* (c. 1563) wears black with silver sleeves and trim, the under garment moulded like armour over the extensive belly; and Gheeraerts II's *Unknown Lady in Red* (1620) is in embroidered orange velvet and grey silk garments with wide lace cuffs. The relevance of these portraits to costumes worn by pregnant characters on the Jacobethan stage is a confirmation of a celebration of the pregnant body, and the desire to richly dress it.

2 The Gravid Body: Juliet, *Measure for Measure*

Juliet in *Measure for Measure*, a play first performed in 1604 when violent and dark plays gained popularity, is one of Shakespeare's two roles calling for visible pregnancy. Her near-term pregnancy sets the plot in action: an old law banning unmarried sex has been revived by Angelo, acting as the absent Duke's deputy, and the crime's punishment is death. Though Juliet and Claudio are secretly betrothed (a pledge as serious as marriage) the young lovers are found guilty of lechery by Angelo and imprisoned, Claudio scheduled for beheading the next day, and Juliet's death (presumably) delayed until after giving birth. The story is set in a darkly sexualized, degenerate Vienna, riddled (the play is full of syphilitic references) with corruption at all levels, and mismanaged by the ruling Duke. The Duke's central presence has a 'murky stage history'.[17] His earlier incarnation as a quasi-religious figure has been reinterpreted in productions since the mid twentieth century, including those discussed here, where directors and actors have placed greater emphasis on his, and other characters', psychology and the effects (mainly negative) of political power.[18] Juliet is one of the play's few innocents, as is Claudio's sister Isabella, whose attempts to save her brother's life by pleading passionately with Angelo, unwittingly incites the deputy's lust.

---

[17] Allam, 1993, 'The Duke in *Measure for Measure*' in *Players of Shakespeare 3*. 21–41. Allam played the Duke in the 1987 RSC production.

[18] Productions discussed: 1950 RSC, dir. Peter Brook; 1970 RSC dir. John Barton; 1987 RSC, dir. Nicholas Hytner; 1991, dir. Peter Zadek, Odéon, Paris; 1994 RSC, dir. Steven Pimlott; 2013–19, Cheek by Jowl and Pushkin Theatre, dir. Declan Donnellan, livestream performance, 2017.

Juliet's role is small, but her situation haunts the shadows of the main story, Isabella's struggle. Shakespeare sketches in Juliet through other characters' comments: she is respectfully referred to as 'Madam Juliet' (1.2.111); she is held as dearly as a cousin by the intensely moral Isabella (1.4.45-50); and the prison's Provost is concerned about her as a prisoner who is 'a gentlewoman of mine' (2.3.10). She and Claudio are the play's purest lovers, but are still tainted by the city's corruption. Their engagement is secretive; Claudio says the 'stealth of our most mutual entertainment / With character too gross is writ on Juliet' (1.2.149-50) and Pompey, the bawdy house tapster, observes that Claudio has been 'groping for trout in a peculiar river' (1.2.87). Juliet appears in three scenes (1.2, 2.3, 5.1) and only speaks briefly in one, 2.3. In 1.2 she and Claudio are put on public display, paraded through the city as they are taken to prison. The lovers' helplessness as prisoners has been staged with various methods of restraint, including manacled wrists, arms pinned behind the back or held in front, often with a noose around the neck with ropes held by police. For this scene Juliet's costume, almost always, includes a visible pregnancy and, generally, is in keeping with the production's design and her status as a gentlewoman. One exception was Peter Brook who did not include Juliet's expected gravid body in his 1950 production, designed by Brook when he was not using pregnancy costumes in his stripped-down, innovative productions. His Juliet (Hazel Penwarden) was dressed in a simple Elizabethan/Jacobean gentlewoman's dress, slim-waisted with no sign of pregnancy. This was very similar to, or possibly the same, costume the pregnant Hermione wore in his *Winter's Tale* the next year. Versions of *Measure for Measure* have been costumed in approximations of nearly every period from Renaissance to modern, though latterly Freud's Vienna, 1930s Germany, and Margaret Thatcher's 1970s England have been popular. Nicholas Hytner's 1987 RSC production, designed by Mark Thompson, is typical; his costumes were twentieth century, of no particular era, but with a sharp demarcation between high and low social levels. Putting Juliet and Claudio in some form of prison clothes at the beginning is always a possibility. For example, Peter Zadek dressed the couple in pinned-together stiffened pieces of immaculately white paper or fabric, suggesting penitential garments worn over their ordinary clothes. The whiteness of that covering was ironic as the prison was a house of torture, some of it violently enacted on stage.

Juliet's second scene 2.3 takes place in prison, and is a (supposedly) religious interview with a friar, actually Duke Vincentio in disguise. The range of costume choices made by directors and designers here has been very wide. It includes a simple white smock in John Barton's 1970 RSC production, designed by Timothy O'Brien, and an equally plain long white robe in Nicholas Hytner's 1991, RSC, with both garments remaining white in the final scene. Darker interpretations have included costumes in coarser fabrics, even filthy rags. In Declan Donnellan's modern dress versions, co-produced by Cheek by Jowl and the Pushkin Theatre, Moscow, performed internationally in Russian during 2013–2019, designed by Nick Ormerod, the extremely pregnant prisoner Juliet (Anastasia Lebedeva) wore a modern smock top and trousers of a coarse grey fabric, designed to emphasize her large pregnancy. The top curved over the extended belly that hampered her as she tried to sit down, accomplished by leaning back and slowly lowering herself onto the chair set beside the Provost's desk. When seated, the slope of her body made the belly dominate her silhouette. Her responses to the Friar/Duke's questions were balanced between acceptance of guilt and pride. This was a rather muddled Friar, faking his way through a blessing (sign of the cross, hand on her head and offering his hand to be kissed) who forgot to remove his ducal ring, which Juliet could not miss. Flustered by this mistake, he let slip that Claudio was to be executed. In the time it took for Juliet to register the news, he disappeared and she turned her fury on the Provost seated behind the desk beside her. In her outrage the big belly was forgotten as she climbed on the desk and began slapping him. The clean-cut young officer stopped her attack by embracing and kissing her as the scene ended in a blackout. This seemed less a sexual threat to her than his only solution for dealing with a hysterical young woman. Later, but before the final scene, she wandered across the stage, holding Claudio's rolled up jacket under her arm and crying out in labour pains.[19]

Directors have also used this prison interview scene to make it clear that despite the vulnerability of the pregnancy Juliet has been treated roughly in prison. An early example of this is Steven Pimlott's 1994 RSC staging,

---

[19] The livestream recording can be viewed as part of CbJ's educational program; www.cheekbyjowl.com.

designed by Ashley Martin-Davies, which also demonstrated how deeply the part can be enfolded into a production, here as an emblem of a sadistic police state. Juliet (Monica Dolan) is absent from the first act, and her first appearance is in prison where her battered appearance was unexpected and shocking. She was dirty, gagged, in shock, covered with bruises, one eye swollen shut, and wore a filthy rag of a smock.[20] Learning of Claudio's sentence, she collapsed, struggled with the police officers (a man and woman) who dragged the screaming Juliet away. Her screams continued to penetrate from off stage. Unusually, she was also present as an observer during the final scene, sitting in the shadows in the gallery that curved around the upper back wall. A policewoman sat beside her, at times putting a comforting (and possibly restraining) arm around her shoulder. On the revelation that Claudio was alive, she walked down the stairs and sat beside him. She was still pregnant and the only change was that her face and body were clean. The lovers were both shattered by their treatment.

Pimlott's reunion of the lovers in Juliet's silent third and final scene was a familiar staging, although her continuing pregnancy was unusual. Her presence is expected here, and she often enters with the other prisoners, though some editions of the play do not indicate when or if she appears. For example, A. R. Braunmuller's Arden Shakespeare edition omits it, but does include her on the chart of characters present in the act. She often appears holding her new born baby. In Hytner's production she and Claudio were in the background cooing over their infant while the undecided Isabella faced the Duke who was waiting for an answer to his marriage proposal. In Donnellan's version, Claudio ignored Isabella who threw herself at his feet, heard the baby's cry, walked over to Juliet (now freshly dressed), and embraced her. In the final moments music began and the new parents danced, twirling around the stage with the baby in their arms. After hesitation Angelo and Mariana also danced and eventually, and rather stiffly so did the Duke and Isabella.

With *Measure for Measure* the pattern of costume choices (though not the design) is well established, dictated by Juliet's few appearances, and

---

[20] The RSC archive at the Shakespeare Birthplace Trust has two production photographs with explicit details.

informed by her social identity and her pregnancy. In contrast the next play discussed here, *All's Well That Ends Well*, offers the director and designer a unique opportunity to include a visible pregnancy or omit it. The choices are different in every production, and no particular pattern seems to emerge from the mixed bag of decisions of how to stage the play's notoriously open-ended closing scene.

3 Choosing Visibility: Helena, *All's Well That Ends Well*

The option to include a visible pregnancy occurs in the final twenty-nine lines before the Epilogue (5.3.305-34) of *All's Well That Ends Well*, in one of Shakespeare's 'irrational endings', where Helena (thought to be dead) reappears and announces her pregnancy to the husband who abandoned her.[21] Earlier, in protest to his forced marriage to Helena, Bertram, Count of Roussillon left her after setting two seemingly impossible tasks that she must complete before he is willing to be her husband. These are: when she has the ring 'which shall never leave' his finger and when she can 'show' him a child that he is father to 'begotten of thy body' (3.2.55-57). Determined to be with Bertram, Helena accomplishes both tasks. (In the story believed to be Shakespeare's source, when they reunite she has twin boys in her arms.) It is assumed that Helena's claim to pregnancy is the truth. The play makes it clear that the ring was obtained in Florence, and the impregnation occurred through a 'bed trick' where Helena substituted herself for another woman, the Widow's daughter, Diana. Whether or not Helena needs to be shown with a gravid body as proof of pregnancy is not specified, so it is a production's choice. No one in the scene refers to a visible pregnancy. Diana says he has 'got his wife with child' [and she] 'feels her young one kick' (5.3.301-2). There is no indication, however, of how much time has

---

[21] The plot: Helena is the orphaned daughter of a physician, obsessively in love with Bertram the son of her protectress the Countess of Roussillon; Helena cures the King of France of a painful fistula; her reward is to choose Bertram as her husband; he objects to a forced marriage beneath his status and leaves France. Scene 5.3 includes, among others, Bertram, the Countess, the King, and, from Florence, the Widow and her daughter Diana.

passed between the encounter in Italy and Helena's return to France; this makes the pregnancy prosthesis' size optional. In 5.1 Helena is en route and refers to travelling fast, with 'exceeding posting day and nights (5.1.1). That could mean either that she returned as soon as the pregnancy was definite, or waited until near term before hurrying back to France, to give the birth in her own country.

There is no specific performance history of Helena in a pregnancy costume, as there is for Juliet in *Measure for Measure* and Hermione in *The Winter's Tale*. It is unlikely that it was included before the early 1950s in twentieth-century productions, and probably was not present in nineteenth-century productions which tended to feature a sentimental Helena in a reduced role and an unconditionally 'happy' ending.[22] In 5.3, the presence of the King and Countess makes this a public/private scene where Bertram can neither deny nor attack Helena's claims. When she announces the tasks completed, Bertram tells the King that if she can 'make me know this clearly, / I'll love her dearly, ever, ever dearly' (5.3, 315-16). If she is visibly pregnant, there is the consideration of how a director or actor would use these lines. There is enough ambiguity in the character, and his relations with Helena, to make this promise unreliable. The play's ending has become thought of as ambiguous, and the couple's future together as unsettled. A visibly pregnant Helena is a significant example of performing pregnancy in Shakespeare's plays, but its inclusion does not necessarily have a definitive effect on either Helena's or Bertram's behaviour. Over the past fifty years, the number of productions including a visibly pregnant Helena and those omitting the device is equally balanced, and there is no clear pattern of what happens with the ending when visibility is used. A gravid body is not a guarantee that Helena and Bertram will respond in a specific way, but it and the ending have become increasingly central issues. They are cited in the first sentences of Diane Lowman's *Shakespeare Newsletter* review of the RSC's 2022 production. Her second sentence begins: 'A very pregnant Helena and a very discombobulated Bertram stood alone on stage .... a yard apart', and 'tentatively touching fingers' they 'exchange

---

[22] Early twentieth-century UK productions including those by: F. R.Benson, 1916; William Poel, 1920–21; W. Bridge Adams, 1922; Barry Jackson, 1927; Robert Atkins, 1921–22, 1940.

inscrutable gazes of, what?'[23] Whether Helena is visibly pregnant or not, Bertram's reactions are unpredictable, which is one reason they are carefully observed by reviewers who have noted that he has: embraced her, rejected her, been amazed, puzzled, angry, indifferent, or even intrigued. The visible pregnancy does make possible staging a surprise reveal. In Peter Hall's 1982 production with elegant Louis XIV costumes designed by John Gunter, Helena (Sophie Thompson), entered wearing a cloak and, keeping her back to the audience, knelt beside Bertram who was facing the King upstage; it was only when she stood and turned front that her advanced pregnancy was revealed. Hall's Bertram sounded convincing when he pledged himself to her and held out his hand, which he had refused to do at the wedding. Here the large pregnancy made Helena sympathetic, but in other productions, including McIntire's discussed below, it has made her seem controlling, callously throwing her pregnant belly in Bertram's (possibly horrified) face. Audiences have seen endings that are happy, unhappy, hesitant, indecisive, and have included reluctant reconciliations and rejections. The couple has left the stage walking closely together or in various degrees of separation. They have also remained alone on stage staring at each other with a range of emotions, but frequently, simply inscrutable.

In any production, there is one important thing a pregnancy costume consistently achieves: everyone knows that Helena is pregnant. This does not necessarily connect one production to another, nor to a specific theatrical trend, as seen in darker versions of Juliet's treatment in *Measure for Measure*. Nor does it speak to current social attitudes toward pregnant bodies as seen in the costume history of *The Winter's Tale*. In *All's Well*, directors have opted for a visibly pregnant Helena for various combinations of reasons, and an in-depth discussion of their choices and usage requires a more detailed exploration than can be included here. Nevertheless, a brief sketch of the play's final scene in a few productions is indicative of how it has worked. To start with, two examples featuring visible pregnancy, one mid twentieth century, the other recent, have very different endings. In both, what Helena wears as maternity clothing makes a difference. This is particularly true in Tyrone Guthrie's productions, in 1953 at the Ontario Shakespeare Festival and in 1959 at the

---

[23] http://shakespearenewsletter.com>alls-not-well-a-review; no date.

Shakespeare Memorial Theatre in Stratford-upon-Avon, both with costumes by Tanya Moiseiwitsch. The Edwardian setting was Guthrie's innovation and, where appropriate, Moiseiwitsch's costumes for men and women were elegant. Helena (Irene Worth in Ontario, Zoe Caldwell in Stratford-upon-Avon) entered the final scene preceded by soft music. She was fully pregnant, gorgeously dressed in a frothy pastel-coloured gown with layers of organza and silk. The style was similar to Dior's 1950s couture ball gowns, but not out of place with the production's take on Edwardian dress. Its effect on Bertram was dramatic: he fell to his knees in front of her, embraced her, and placed his face on her belly. Although this enthusiasm sounds surprising, there had been previous indications of his attraction to her. In the husband-choosing dance he took her hand voluntarily, dropping it only when the King insisted he call her wife, and in a post-wedding scene invented by Guthrie, he appeared tender and dazed in contrast to the harsh words he spoke.[24] The gown had transformed Helena from the first act's orphan, wearing a dress appropriate for an upper-level servant, into a polished, sophisticated, and beautiful woman who melted Bertram's icy snobbishness. The final reconciliation was as uncomplicated as those of the previous century's sentimental versions.

Seventy years later, the RSC's most recent production, directed by Blanche McIntyre, updated the play to the present: The *Guardian*'s review, 'Problem play gets tasty Gen Z makeover', applauded the update (Anfa Akbbar, 26 August 2022) and praised Rosie Sheehy's Helena for standing apart as a 'force to be reckoned with'. The production included innumerable messages on cell phones, a Rave in Florence, and a French court where young men dressed in brightly coloured, possibly expensive, leisure clothing. A hint of different generational expectations emerged in the *Observer* review (Clare Brennan, 28 August 2022) which found this an uneven, 'unromantic, social media-inflected production' and Sheehy's Helena 'brisk and determined'. In interviews McIntyre spoke of her dislike of the play, its characters, and her decidedly contemporary approach.[25] The only explanation the director could find for the characters' behaviour, especially Helena's obsession with Bertram,

---

[24] See John Russell Brown, 'The Year's Contribution to Shakespeare Studies.' *Shakespeare Survey 13*, 140–42.

[25] See *Stratford Herald* interview by Gill Saunders, 7 September 2022.

was that they were very young. Robert Innes Hopkins' modern dress designs captured this attitude in Helena's costumes. In her early scenes, including those with the French King, she was dressed in a version of a messy school uniform that consisted of an oversized shapeless jacket, a frumpy dress, and tie up shoes worn with ankle socks. For the awkward wedding she looked miserable in a schoolgirl's idea of a white bridal dress with a short veil. She was wearing the same or a similar school dress on her return, now pregnant, to France. McIntyre's very clever choice for the visible pregnancy was to have the 'bump' slightly visible when Helena was about to leave Florence, and fully developed when she arrived in Roussillon. In a world very different from Guthrie's *All's Well*, the visible pregnancy added to the alienation between Bertram and Helena and at the end, they stood alone, silently facing one another, with no indication that this could work well.

Two RSC productions that took the middle path are Trevor Nunn's in 1981 and Nancy Meckler's in 2013. Nunn's production was set somewhere between the end of the Edwardian age and the First World War, and had strong Shavian naturalist overtones.[26] The intelligent Helena (Harriet Walter) was not visibly pregnant, but in the final scene her costume gave her the slightly rounded softness that can accompany the early months of a pregnancy. The costume was stylish, in a soft pale pink fabric and suitable for a Lady. The scene's ending was enigmatic, its mood underscored by Guy Woolfenden's cello music. Helena and Bertram were left alone tentatively touching hands. Stanley Wells noted that there 'is still no kiss', but 'A precarious rapport has been achieved: the ending may also be a beginning' (*TLS*, 27 November 1981). Walter later wrote that she 'tried to make Helena as palatable' as she possibly could. She could not believe that Shakespeare meant to leave the audience with a sense that the marriage would not last or that Bertram 'was saddled with a domineering woman'. Instead, she thought he meant 'to leave us with a feeling that these two people have gone on an incredible journey' and might work it out in 'an interesting life together'.[27]

---

[26] From the early 1900s, Helena had often been played as though she was a George Bernard Shaw heroine, an independent 'New Woman'. Walter's interpretation was in this style.

[27] Walter, 2016, *Brutus and Other Heroines*, London: Nick Hern Books, 20.

In 2013, Nancy Meckler included a 'big-belly' and an ending that focused on Helena's close relationship with the Countess. Michael Billington wrote in his overview of 'the best' productions of *All's Well* (*Guardian* 25 April 2014): 'I still cherish memories of the Guthrie version, but Meckler's was the best of modern times' and praised its 'distinctly feminist reading'. Katrina Lindsay's costumes were modern dress, of no particular time but suggesting the 1940s or 50s.[28] Helena's (Joanna Horton) clothing did not indicate mourning; her first dress was graceful, but not fashionable, pale in colour, the skirt trimmed with a black band, and her second dress was red for the French court and was worn for the wedding. In Florence, she wore a nurse's uniform, a long white dress, and a scarf around her head. Her final costume's very rounded pregnancy was emphasized in a clinging dress in white, topped by a sheer, embroidered overdress. Bertram's interest in her had been made clear earlier with his passionate kiss in the wedding scene. When they were reunited in Rossillon, the more unexpected reaction was the rejection by the Countess of her son. When he tried to join her and Helena, she folded her hands and ignored him. Bertram returned to centre stage, held out his hand to Helena who hesitated for a moment then joined him and placed his hand on her belly. Although the aforementioned performances seem to link a visible pregnancy with a reconciliation, the larger range of productions does not support this, even though the idea is intriguing.

4 Case Study: Hermione, *The Winter's Tale*

> One reason why actors' accounts of their performance experiences interest us is that they can connect with aspects of the plays – including the emotional response – that seem inaccessible to much literary criticism.
>
> Lois Potter[29]

---

[28] See: 'Designing the Countess| All's Well That Ends Well; www.rsc.org.uk>nancy-meckler-2013-production

[29] Potter, 2014, 167.

The story of the actresses who played Hermione in nineteenth-century productions of *The Winter's Tale* is one of independent women, earning their living on the stage, arranging costumes which they used to create the character, but even more importantly their professional identity. Their voices, sometimes as clamorous as modern actors', are found in their memoirs, correspondence, and biographies.

The London theatres reopened in 1660, but there were no major full-length versions of *The Winter's Tale* until 1802.[30] The major objections to the play in the eighteenth century were its lack of classical unity in time and place, and its mix of comedy and tragedy. Moreover, Shakespeare's characters did not fit comfortably into established categories. Leontes' actions lack nobility, and his morbid jealousy is neither heroic nor tragic. Hermione, though noble, is not a tragic heroine doomed to die. Opportunities to stage the play in London were also limited. Only the two theatres with royal patents (Drury Lane and Covent Garden) were licensed to produce serious spoken drama, including Shakespeare. Other theatres were allowed to present adaptations of these works if they included a specific amount of music and dance. This was easily done by featuring the shepherd-filled Bohemia scenes as a country festival. There were several adaptations of the play as pastoral, including *The Sheep Shearing* (1754), that focused on the bucolic love story of a prince and a princess raised as a shepherd's daughter. David Garrick's *Florizel and Perdita* (first performance 1753, published 1756) set the action in Bohemia, but moved back to Sicilia for the fifth-act statue scene, with Leontes and Hermione given extra lines written by Garrick. This three-act version of *The Winter's Tale* was the predominate text used between 1756 and the end of the century.[31] Its popularity helps explain the existence of a number of pictures of actresses as Hermione in similar poses: standing, leaning an arm on a pedestal, wearing a diaphanous semi-formal contemporary robe. Garrick's additional

---

[30] Hermione has four scenes: 1.2, happily married, mother of Mamillius, expecting a second child; 2.1, mistakenly attacked by husband Leontes for adultery with Polixenes, arrested; 3.2 on trial after giving birth in prison, faints when told her son has died, pronounced dead; 5.2, 16 years later, appears as a statue which comes to life, forgives Leontes, united with daughter.

[31] Shattuck, 1974, 184.

lines extended Leontes' reaction to the statue and added to the amount of time the actress must not move. The pedestal, originally placed there to help her stay steady, became the character's iconic stage property.[32]

Revival: Sarah Siddons 1802–1811

The Winter's Tale with a relatively complete text was revived by actor-manager John Philip Kemble's (1757–1823) production at the Drury Lane Theatre, 25 March 1802, with Hermione played by Kemble's acting partner and sister, Sarah Siddons (1755–1831).[33] When Siddons spoke Hermione's: 'I had thought, sir, to have held my peace' (1.2.27) it was the first recorded occasion since the 1630s that an audience heard these words in a professional performance. Kemble's *Winter's Tale* was spectacularly produced, designed to satisfy a growing preference for lavish sets, costumes, and technological advances in stagecraft. The first scene was set in an ancient Grecian square, the remaining Sicilia scenes were played in a Tudor setting.[34] This was her first performance of Hermione, and the production showcased Siddons' strengths: it emphasized the tragic and minimized the comic. The *Evening Mail* is representative of the enthusiastic critical reception: the play was 'brought forward in almost every respect, with a judgement and attention that are highly credible to the Manager [Kemble]' and 'The Hermione of Mrs. Siddons towers above all praise' (26 March 1802).

Playing Hermione marked an important point in Siddons' long career. She had acted many of Shakespeare's women, including Lady Macbeth, Constance in *King John*, and Queen Katherine in *Henry VIII*. For decades she triumphed in tragedy, but she also continued to keep roles that were no longer suitable. Now middle-aged, she had become too old and, some complained, too stout for many of her signature roles, including Juliet and Rosalind. Introducing Hermione offered a satisfying challenge with

---

[32] The 1856 photograph of Ellen Kean in the trial scene costume has her standing next to a pedestal, Hermione's usual prop for the statue scene, but she wore Greek robes as a statue.

[33] Siddons' Hermione in 1775 was not Shakespeare's; it was in *The Distressed Mother*; see Asleson, 1999, xiii.

[34] Bartholomeusz, 1982, 48.

a suitably dignified part, a Shakespeare role she had never played, costumes suitable to her matronly shape, and the opportunity to put into practice costume reforms. Nina H. Kennard points out in *Mrs Siddons* (1893) that Hermione was among the actresses' 'greatest successes' and 'was more suited to her age and appearance than others that she undertook in late life'.[35]

Kemble's commitment to grandeur included costumes that were imaginatively based on historic art and artefacts, instead of the usual practice of dressing all characters in contemporary clothing. For Siddons' first scenes Hermione was wrapped in richly coloured robes, probably in the Tudor style and repurposed from her performance that season as Queen Katherine in Shakespeare's *Henry VIII*. This meant that Hermione's visible pregnancy could be dressed with decorum in a historically inspired garment, discretely suited to her mature figure. The costume would have approximated late pregnancy through padding or simply by shaping the robes to create the correct silhouette. After years of costumes hiding her own pregnancies from audiences, in her last major role Siddons needed to make it clear to the audience that this character was about to give birth.[36] Her costume would have co-ordinated with Kemble's own as Leontes in the first act: a velvet and gold mantle, a blue and gold dress and a gold coronet with white plumes.[37] But Siddons would have arranged what she wore with an eye on Regency taste, and put into practice her reform of tragedy costumes to end 'the enormous head-gear and hoops and flounces of the previous day.[38] In her *Reminiscences*, the actress writes about her preference in her own clothing for a more natural look that was without stays, avoided fashionably dressed powdered hair and overly decorated dresses.[39] Siddons' costumes recorded in drawings and paintings, including Joshua Reynold's *Sarah Siddons as Tragic Muse* (1774) trace her transition toward this simpler style, and her preferences were very much in tune with fashion.[40]

---

[35] Kennard, 1893, 199. [36] Asleson, 1999, viii. [37] See Bartholomeusz, 1982, 49.
[38] Odell, 1920, 1966, 93, vol 2. [39] Siddons, *Reminiscences*, printed 1942.
[40] See Asleson, 1999.

Although the third act's trial scene would have made use of Siddons' skill in tragedy, it was her appearance in the statue scene that received the most attention in print. This would have been a scene familiar from Garrick's adaptation, *Florizel and Perdita*. Kemble's innovation was to present Hermione as a classically dressed Grecian statue instead of the fashionable déshabillé gowns seen in eighteenth-century actresses' images.[41] Siddons' Hermione resembled the ancient statues that archaeologists were sending to London for exhibition, and Kemble's version of the statue scene evoked the Hellenic world through a mix of archaeology and fashionable art. The public's interest in Greek and Roman remains had been growing since expanded excavations of Pompeii in the mid eighteenth century. Archaeological discoveries would continue to feed this interest. Regency fashion had already accustomed the public eye to dresses in slim columns, with short sleeves and bared arms, and Hermione's statue costume, copied from antiquity, would have been simple to create. It only needed a supple fabric with enough substance to drape in deep folds, making it seem as much as possible as if it were carved from marble. On Siddons the effect was dramatic. Thomas Campbell says she 'shewed great beauty of head, neck, shoulders, and arms that Praxiteles might have studied'.[42] James Boaden, who saw one of her *Winter's Tale* performances, recalled in 1825 that she was 'one of the noblest statues that even Grecian taste ever invented. The figure posed something like one of the muses in profile. The drapery was ample in its folds and seemingly stony in its texture'.[43] Those seemingly stony folds were actually highly flammable muslin that surrounded her. Siddons described in a letter how she was nearly 'terminated' when 'my drapery flew over the lamps that were placed behind my pedestal' and, except for the quick action of a stagehand, they would have 'run like

---

[41] The *Dictionary of Fashion History* defines déshabillé as: 'Period 1703-19th century. Dressed in a negligent or careless manner or a style of dress to indicate such casual attitudes'.

[42] Campbell, 1834, vol 2, 265.   [43] Boaden, 1827, vol 2, 314.

wildfire'.[44] This costume is evoked in the Westminster Abbey and Paddington Green monuments that celebrate Siddons' career and present her as a classical statue.

Transition: Helen Faucit (Lady Martin) 1837

From Sarah Siddons onwards, the role of Hermione has generally been played by women in their thirties or forties; Ellen Terry was fifty-two when she played her for the first time. A major exception to the trend is Helen Faucit (1817–1898) who was only twenty when she played Hermione in Willian Charles Macready's production at Covent Garden in 1837. Macready (1793–1873), the 'Eminent Tragedian', was a dramatic force in early Victorian theatre, known for his Shakespeare productions, the patronage of Queen Victoria, his commitment to raising the level of national culture, and his 'strenuous endeavours to advance the drama as a branch of national literature and art'.[45] Macready attempted to revive Shakespeare's popularity in the manner of Kemble, including using some of his sets and costumes. He hired Faucit, despite her youthfulness, as the company's leading actress to take on many of the roles played by Siddons. Faucit's career is carefully documented in Carol Jones Carlyle's biography (2000); also given a useful but hagiographic account in the biography/memoir by her husband Sir Theodore Martin (1900); and discussed by herself in a collection of essays about her Shakespeare roles: Ophelia, Portia, Desdemona, Juliet, Imogen, Rosalind, Beatrice, and, in the second edition, Hermione (1891).[46] Her comments on Hermione's pregnancy are a mix of Victorian sentimentality (the book is dedicated to the Queen) and ideas that are as modern as the conversations of today's actors. Faucit is deeply romantic about marriage and motherhood, both of which she had experienced. She writes of Hermione's 'years of happy wedlock' and points out that in productions it is always the left hand that she gives to Leontes, 'the one with the wedding ring'.[47]

---

[44] Kennard, 1893, 200 quotes from the letter; the entire bottom of the dress' train was burned.

[45] See Trewin, 1971, xi–xxiv, 89–165.

[46] Carlyle, 2000; Sir Theodore Martin, 1900; Helena Faucit, Lady Martin, 1891.

[47] Faucit, 1891, 344.

She sounds very modern when describing how during performances she imagined what Hermione's thoughts 'would be about the baby she was carrying'. She imagined, and perhaps used this in performance, that Hermione was 'suddenly reminded by a painful throb of her impending trial [and] affrighted by the thought that jailors are to be her sole attendants' at the birth.[48]

Although Faucit was a member of a theatrical family,[49] and was experienced on stage, her first performance of Hermione, when she was twenty, was heavily controlled by Macready whose 'will was law'.[50] His style could be overly theatrical. Her description of an incident in their first performance of the statute scene gives a sense of his acting method. Her costume would have been a version of Siddons' Grecian statue and included, as she says, a veil covering her 'bound' hair. Faucit recalled that when Hermione came to life and stepped down from the dais, 'his passionate joy seemed beyond control; now he was prone at my feet, then embracing me and caressing the unbound hair that escaped from beneath the veil'. When she shrieked in surprise, Macready whispered to her: 'Don't be frightened, my child! Don't be frightened!'[51] This is a much-quoted story, used to demonstrate the passionate intensity of Macready's acting style, but it also includes a useful costume note. Macready's Shakespeare productions copied Kemble's as much as possible, so Hermione's costumes would have been influenced by his ideas of what Siddons wore, including Tudor robes for her first two scenes. Faucit would have been responsible for adding the pregnancy's shape. She described how earlier that season her mother helped her pad out a costume to give her Queen Katherine in *Henry VIII* (a famous Siddons role) a matronly shape. She may have done something similar for Hermione, definitely necessary to create the pregnancy curve. Her husband remembers 'her distinction of manner, and the power as well as pathos of

---

[48] Faucit, 1891, 352, 360.

[49] Her sister Harriet played Paulina to Ellen Tree's Hermione in Macready's 1835 *Winter's Tale;* Bartholmeusz's appendix lists H. Faucit in that production as Paulina and H. Faucit as Hermione in 1837, without noting they are different actresses.

[50] Carlyle, 2000, 57. [51] Martin, 1900, 48–49, quoting Faucit's letter.

her acting, triumphed over the disadvantages of her youth, which no ingenuity of dress could conceal'.[52]

Later she continued to use antique dress in her own productions. Working independently from Macready, the actress staged revivals of *Antigone* (1843) and *Iphigenia in Aulis* (1846). Various photographs and Sir Frederick Williams Burton's drawings show her in costumes copied from Greek statues. The chiton and mantle are beautifully draped to display her 'heroically proportioned limbs' and 'potent combination of physical and spiritual appeal'.[53] Her memoir, covering a career that spanned nearly a century, starts with an artistic inheritance from an eighteenth-century actress, and ends with a perceptive discussion of Shakespeare's women at the end of that century.

Ancient World: Ellen Kean 1856 and Ellen Terry 1906

The first time Ellen Kean (1805–1880) played Hermione was in Macready's 1835 *Winter's Tale*, the next time was twenty years later. This was the 1856 production by her husband Charles Kean (1811–1868) at the Princess's Theatre, London, which he managed from 1850 to 1859, and where the couple made a speciality of Shakespeare productions.[54] Success was based on a combination of a relatively full text and spectacular staging. The 'revival' (his preferred term) of *The Winter's Tale* was lavish: a cast of over 170 extras, 500 costumes, special effects made possible by new technology, and every detail presented with as much historical accuracy as possible. Responding to critical complaints about excessive detail, he defended his staging as 'recreation wherein instruction is blended with amusement'.[55] Kean satisfied audiences' increasing taste for spectacle but made it respectable.

Given Kean's obsession with archaeological accuracy, it is impressive that his wife succeeded in refusing to conform with her costumes. But, according to Ellen Terry, she was in many ways 'the leading spirit in the

---

[52] Martin, 1900, 44. [53] Carlyle, 2000, 145–48.

[54] In their final season at the Princess's, 242 of the 250 performances were Shakespeare.

[55] Kean, 1856, 'Historical Notes'.

theatre; at the least, a joint ruler, not a queen-consort'.[56] The Keans' *Winter's Tale* was done as a 'Greek play with Greek dresses, Greek customs, and Greek architecture'.[57] The exception was Ellen's costumes which she insisted on adapting to suit her own sense of propriety. This is not the situation of an eighteenth-century actress insisting on being modishly fashionable, but of a nineteenth-century woman maintaining fashionable decorum. Nevertheless, Ellen Kean chose to wear a visibly pregnant costume that fitted closely to the mid-section of the body and emphasized its bulky shape. The pregnancy was realistic in size and form and very much of her devising. The style of the dress and the pattern of its decorations were loosely adapted from a vase painting, 'The Marriage of Hercules and Hebe'.[58] It is the only one of her three costumes that Kean included in his 'Historical Notes' where he listed the sources for thirty-six costumes (major and minor roles) based on ancient painted vases. Hermione's pregnancy costume is a loosely draped garment in a light fabric, with soft folds, a simple neckline, the bodice gathered below the bust. The dress was decorated with dark geometric designs around the hem and down the front. A wide mantle (the Greek *himation*), in similar colour and design, was wrapped close around the body, and highlighted the pregnancy's shape with its border decoration forming a diagonal line across the belly.[59] Three bracelets added a historic note (one worn high up on a bare arm, and one on each wrist), and so did the wreath of flowers around her head, which Kean

---

[56] Terry, 1908, 11. [57] Hardwick, 1954, 33.

[58] Kean, 1856, cites the source as: 'From a Painted Vase in the Royal Museum at Berlin, representing the Marriage of Hercules and Hebe. Engraved in Gerhard's Vases Apuliens, taf. 15'.

[59] www.library.harvard.edu, Hollis Archival Discovery, MS Thr 905, Charles John Kean and cast collection, Digital Material, Ellen Kean nos. 32, 33. 34; V&A: www.vam.ac.uk, search for 'Ellen Kean in Guy Little Collection'. Hermione costumes are not labelled, but can be identified by previous descriptions. The pregnancy is not visible in this seated portrait, (GLCVII.iii.1) but costume details, including the chaplet, are clear. The Royal Collection Trust has the glass negative of the pregnancy costume photograph, www.rct.uk.collection.mrs-charles-kean. The site also has the carte de visite photograph of her in the statue costume.

explained was patterned on the chaplets worn in the ancient world on festive occasions.[60] In the final act Hermione appeared as the classic Greek statue dressed in a chiton (or peplos), made of a white fabric heavy enough to suggest carved marble. In the third act's trial scene she wore a regal costume that was closer to the Victorian style than the ancient Grecian. Made of dark coloured fabric, it had a simple long-sleeved bodice, a broad skirt, and referenced the ancient world with a wide mantle in the same fabric and colour, draped loosely across the body in the style of a toga. Her only ornament was the circlet of gold leaves on her head.[61] This photograph is frequently used as an illustration, but not identified as the trial scene.[62] The pose is confusing and suggests the statue because Hermione is standing by a pedestal, the prop seen in late seventeenth- and early eighteenth-century pictures of Hermione as statue. (The tradition started by Garrick.[63]) The costume has no indication of the horrors endured by Hermione giving birth in prison, but the previous scene's set included a backdrop of a terrifying medieval prison. All three costumes can be seen in photographs. Harvard's Houghton Library has a series of three printed as *cartes de visite* produced to be sold as souvenirs, distributed as gifts, or used for publicity.[64] In them Ellen Kean's costumes tell the story of the actress's independent shaping of her role, which included dressing Hermione with a deep commitment to current standards of propriety, including starched petticoats under all her dresses.

At mid nineteenth century and at the height of hoop skirt popularity, many actresses preferred to retain their contemporary stays and modest layers of underpinnings, even in classically styled productions, so Ellen Kean was not alone in keeping at least some of her petticoats. It is unexpected when Ellen Terry, fifty years later, resents Kean's Hermione

---

[60] Kean, 1856, 'Historical Notes'.

[61] Houghton Library, Harvard University, Collection: photographs of Charles John Kean and cast, Ellen Kean V&A. www.vam.ac.uk; search for 'Ellen Kean in Guy Little Collection'. The image (GLCVII.iii.2.1) is the carte de visite photograph.

[62] See Bartholomeusz, 1982, Plate 13,

[63] This has also been misidentified as Mrs. Benson.   [64] See n. 48.

being 'always bunched out by layer upon layer of petticoats, in defiance of the fact that classical parts should not be dressed in a superfluity of raiment', the petticoat.[65] In the three cartes de visite the costumes are not particularly 'grotesque'. Perhaps it was easier for Ellen Kean to do with fewer petticoats in the photographer's studio than on stage. The statues' purely classic white chiton and himation seen in the photograph achieved modesty by using a heavy fabric folded so there was no hint of the shape of her thighs.[66] Terry, who played Mamillius in the production, also objected at the time, at the age of eight, to the difference between costume design and reality in her costume's very unclassical wrinkled pink tights worn under an 'authentic' smock.

Terry continued to resent what other actors do to their costumes. She writes that 'then, [1856] as now, actors and actresses seemed unable to keep their own period and their own individuality out of the clothes directly they got them on their backs'.[67] Nevertheless, that is precisely what Terry herself did when she played Hermione in Beerbohm Tree's 1906 production. Her Hermione costumes had little to do with Tree's production designs, but instead reflected her own commitment to the fashions of the Aesthetic Movement and pre-Raphaelite painters. Terry always maintained control over her costumes by working with her own designer, Alice Comyns-Carr, and dressmaker, Mrs. Nettleship of 58 Wigmore St.[68] For Tree's production Terry's daughter Edith Craig may have worked with her on the costumes. Her pregnancy ensemble combined Aesthetic Movement style and colours (yellow and green) and a reference to Ellen Kean's maternity costume. In Terry's version the very wide mantle was yellow with an intricate pattern woven into the wool. In photographs it looks as soft as a cashmere shawl and drapes toga-style from her shoulder, falling in gentle folds across the

---

[65] Terry, 1908, 14; also in Terry, 1932.

[66] See, for example, statues of Siddons in Westminster Abbey and in Paddington Green.

[67] Quoted in Hardwick, 19.

[68] Mrs. Nettleship had come up with the yarn used to knit the soft chain-mail armour in Lady Macbeth's beetle wing costume worn by Terry in Sargent's painting.

front of her body. It indicates the largeness of the pregnancy without actually outlining the body. The tunic underneath is a deep green, styled with a loosely gathered peasant-style bodice and open neckline.[69] By the time Terry played Hermione, the role had become established as one of Shakespeare's great women. It was also a role where leading actresses had directed their costumes' designs for over a century, and this includes Mary Anderson's staging where she was the producer and played Hermione and Perdita.

An American Hermione in London: Mary Anderson 1887

The popular success of Mary Anderson's 1887 *The Winter's Tale* is impressive as testimony to the drawing power of a celebrity in a popularized version of the play. Anderson was an American actress working as an independent producer, who returned to London for a third season at the Lyceum Theatre to present *The Winter's Tale*. She starred in her own production and was the first performer on record to double Hermione and Perdita. Hermione's pregnancy's shape was made explicit, but softened by the costume's layers as designed by Sir Lawrence Alma-Tadema, a painter specializing in sunlit, romantic images of women in antique dress.[70] Anderson's production was set in the ancient world, very much in the style of Charles Kean's. The production was a popular success, and held the record for the play's longest run until in 1951. The critics, to a man (and they were all men), unanimously hated almost everything about it, applauding only Alma-Tadema's costumes, the grandeur of the sets, and the scene painters' art. They did admire Anderson's beauty, especially her skill at holding statuesque poses, but felt that was not enough to make this a good production, and that Johnston Forbes-Robertson's Leontes was miscast. The critics' objections

---

[69] http://collections.vam.ac.uk/item/O141737/guy-little-theatrical-photograph-photograph-window-grove/. See also Veronica Isaac, 2018, '"A Well-Dressed Actress": Exploring the Theatrical Wardrobe of Ellen Terry' and 2021, '"Re-Dressing the Part": The Scenographic Strategies of Ellen Terry (1847–1928)'. Costume textile details here supplied by Veronica Isaac, personal email.

[70] Alma-Tadema's paintings are easily accessible on line; for his use of colour in ancient dress, see also his costume drawings for Henry Irving's *Coriolanus*, 1901.

make a long list that includes: Anderson's acting, verse speaking, and American accent; her lapses remembering lines; her interpretation of Hermione (underdeveloped) and Perdita (overplayed). The critics remembered Ellen Kean and longed for Sarah Siddons who, based on her reputation, would have known how to perform Hermione. They found the doubling unnecessary, egoistical, and a grave mistake given Anderson's limited talents. They objected to her cuts in the text that included removing two-thirds of Paulina's lines, one of Autolycus' scenes, and all of Time's speeches. They complained about the bowdlerization of Shakespeare's text, even though it differed very little from Kean's. Critics, and much of the audience, found that dropping the curtain every fifteen minutes to create 'tableau scenes' was an annoying interruption that further lengthened a production that also required long intervals for scene changes. And they thoroughly disliked Anderson's overenthusiastic fans who packed the house, cheered when Perdita danced, gave Hermione an ovation for the trial scene, and called her back repeatedly for curtain calls. This was consistently spelled out by reviewers in great detail.[71]

The production was tailored to suit popular taste and was a box office success. To her adoring fans, the actress was a great talent whose production gave them her stunning beauty gorgeously dressed, spectacular staging, and satisfyingly melodramatic acting. They also had the comfort of knowing this was a safe version of *The Winter's Tale*. The text would not offend propriety; Victorian sentiment would be upheld; sexual passion kept at bay; and irony would not be allowed.

Anderson embraced Hermione's pregnancy as a factor in her sentimental portrayal of a mother who showers her young son with kisses, patiently awaits the birth of the next child, and nobly defends herself from false accusations. The *Cassell's Illustrated Shakespeare*, published that year, includes a description of Hermione that coincided with Anderson's interpretation: 'Shakespeare gives Hermione a quiet tenderness and a great patience . . . . [Her] gentle affection

---

[71] Reviews sharing this uniform view in 1887: Sept 10: *Morning Post*; Sept 12: *Times*, *Morning Post*, *Dramatic Review*, *Daily Telegraph*, *Pall Mall Gazette*, *Saturday Review;* Sept 14: *The World*; Sept 15: *Truth*; Sept 16: *The Stage*; Sept. 17: *Era* and *Illustrated Sporting and Dramatic News*.

when attacked by Leontes is patience to the end, with love ever abiding. Love, patience, purity and faith in the powers above, shine through all words and acts of the afflicted queen.'[72] This was captured by Anderson in the nursery scene, which the *Pall Mall Gazette* (12 September 1887) reported was the first to stir up the audience 'to any expression of pleasure'. The report describes the dark room lit by a glowing fire, her ladies playing music, and the 'the stately Hermione, clad in the rather unbecoming red and purple Greek costume, reclining on her couch'. The 'unbecoming red and purple' costume may be the one seen on the cover of the *Illustrated London News* (12 September 1887). Although in black-and-white photographs it looks whiteish, the colour reproduction, possibly for a special edition, tints it purple. The dress evokes the chiton but is composed of layers of tunics, including a bodice that drapes down in deep folds that could suggest pregnancy. The colour reflects fashion's growing preference for the newly invented aniline dyes in bright colours. Also, for this costume, the colour could be claimed as historically accurate based on discoveries of the Tanagras. These fourth-century-BCE polychrome statuettes of 'draped women standing, sitting or dancing' were discovered in the 1870s through tomb excavations in Boeotia, Greece and helped justify the use of coloured clothing in historical paintings of the ancient world.[73]

Anderson's other notable uses of her costumes included the trial scene, where she used a large sheer shawl to completely cover herself when Hermione collapses at hearing Mamillius is dead. In the statue scene, she would have worn something similar to her costume (also designed by Alma-Tadema) for the statue Galatea in W. S. Gilbert's new play *Pygmalion and Galatea* in her first season of renting the Lyceum in 1883.[74] Anderson, using her control as the producer, had overruled Gilbert's preference to stage the play in a modern style. He accepted the classic designs but 'strongly objected to Alma-Tadema's arrangement of her draperies' as too restrictive

---

[72] *Cassell Family Shakespeare*. Charles and Mary Cowden Clark, eds. 1898, 14.

[73] Ribeyrol, Winterbottom, Hewitson, eds. (2024) *Colour Revolution*, 204–11.

[74] See National Gallery: *Mary Anderson (Mrs de Navarro) as Galatea in Pygmalion and Galatea*. Photograph collection x22239, album cabinet card, Henry Van de Weyde photographer. See also by Van de Weyde: Library of Congress, Prints and Photographs, digital ID cph.3b08732, which includes a long shawl.

and too heavily marble, joking that the designer wanted her to even play the role in a marble wig.[75] There were no similar objections in 1887.

London and New York: 'Medievalish-Renaissancy' Costumes 1900's

Mary Anderson's production was the last of the nineteenth-century *Winter's Tale* with elaborately researched sets and props representing the ancient world. The first decade of the twentieth century saw several elegantly produced versions of the play in New York and London. The general preference for sets and costumes was vaguely Renaissance with a touch of medievalism and the aura of the fairy tale books illustrations by Paul Dulac and Arthur Rackham.[76] Hermione continued to be visibly pregnant in 1.2 and 2.1. The Edwardians embraced the romance of childhood that included the angelic mother. There was little connection with contemporary fashion, but the Pre-Raphaelites and the Aesthetic Movement had ignited an interest in a romanticized medieval world that could easily morph into the Italian Renaissance. Good photographic records of Winthrop Ames' New York production show Hermione (Edith Wynne Matthison) in a pregnancy costume that is a simple robe with a long panel of fabric that smoothed the front of the body. This is similar to the Italian *zamorra* favoured by Marie de Medici (1575–1642) during her pregnancies in France.

Between 1894 and 1905, William Poel's Elizabethan Stage Society in London presented Shakespeare's plays on a bare platform designed to replicate the acting conditions of the playwright's own stage. Poel's innovative productions also dressed the actors as they might have been seen by the original audiences and featured versions of Elizabethan and Jacobean dress for all costumes, no matter where or when a play takes place. His goal as an actor-manager was to free Shakespeare productions from the heavy weight of spectacular sets used by Charles Kean and Henry Irving, and return the plays

---

[75] Stedman, 1996, 200.

[76] Between 1904 and 1914 illustrated versions of fairy tales were published first in expensive luxury editions with excellent colour plates that were later more widely sold in popular, less expensive editions. Dulac and Rackham were the genre's leading artists.

to their original simple staging where actors had only the text and costumes to work with. His influence on Shakespeare productions was immense and continues on stage today. On the other hand, his influence on costumes was less effective, but still instrumental in establishing what became a standard hybrid period, identified by Ella Hawkins as 'Jacobethan'.[77] Poel's company did not stage *The Winter's Tale*, so nothing specific was established for dressing Hermione's pregnancy, but his newly established historical style for female costumes was one of the contributors to the gradual flattening out of Hermione's visible pregnancy. Elizabethan/Jacobean dress, as known by Poel, did not offer the material with which to establish a new theatrical convention for a royal queen's 'big-bellied' pregnancy. This absence would later fit comfortably with the mid twentieth century's preference for the disappearance of visible pregnancy. In *Winter's Tale* the slimmer pregnancy costume corresponded to current social practice. Society bracketed off the gravid body, moving it off stage and, literally and figuratively, air brushing it out of the picture. *The Winter's Tale* costumes reflecting this general lack of interest in a pregnant body included Motley's Russian fairy tale costumes in 1948 and Jacques Noël's Hermione's costume in 1960.[78]

Silent Film: Thanhouser 1910

For early film companies Shakespeare represented culture, education, class, and could be strategic in raising films' cultural profile. There were several silent film versions of *The Winter's Tale* by different production companies including: Edison, 1909; Cines, 1910; Thanhouser, 1910, Milano, 1913, and Belle Alliance, 1914. Before becoming a film director, Edwin Thanhouser had thirty years of professional experience in the American theatre during a time when Shakespeare was a staple for any acting company, which may explain why his first two Shakespeare films were the relatively unknown *Winter's Tale* and *Cymbeline* (1913). *The Winter's Tale*, directed by Barry O'Neil, was

---

[77] The term Jacobethan is the central concern in Hawkins, 2022; for Poel, see Hawkins, 21–23.

[78] *The Winters Tale* 1948, directed by Anthony Quayle, Diana Wynyard (Hermione); 1960 director Peter Wood, Elizabeth Sellars (Hermione) both at the Shakespeare Festival Theatre, Stratford-upon Avon.

the first of his company's seven silent Shakespeare films, produced between 1910 and 1916 and an early 'expression of the company's cultural ambitions'.[79] Hermione's visibly pregnant costume in Thanhouser's 1910 film of *The Winter's Tale* is an example of the ways that theatre costumes influence those in early Shakespeare films. In Thanhouser's film (available on DVD) the costumes are a dressing-up-box jumble of times and places. For example, Leontes and Polixenes are in ermine-trimmed robes similar to those in Winthrop Ames' production running at the same time in New York City's New Theatre (only forty-five minutes from Thanhouser's studio).[80] In the film, other members of the court are in a mix of the classical and exotic. The actors use typical silent film gestures and facial expressions, and the play is skilfully adapted. The visibly pregnant Hermione is in keeping with nineteenth-century theatre practices. Although this Hermione is neither as heavily pregnant as Ellen Kean had been in 1856, nor Lillah McCarthy would be in 1912, the pregnancy is clearly indicated, and its importance is emphasized. Hermione (Anna Rosemond) wears a discreet white smock, of no particular period but closer to the Italian Renaissance than ancient Greece. The ancient world of Greek and Rome is suggested by her bare arms with wide bracelets worn above the elbows. The pregnancy is indicated by the fullness of the simple dress and emphasized by the long dark belt worn low to outline her pregnancy's shape. Over the dress she wears an open, full-length, sleeveless garment. On her first appearance she holds this up in front of her, draping it almost in toga-style, but when she walks, laughing and talking with Polixenes, it is open, framing the pregnancy's fullness, but also suggesting something about her easiness in his company. The visible pregnancy is important in telling the story quickly, clearly and silently.

---

[79] For Thanhouser's *The Winter's Tale* see Buchanan 2009, 127,4, (127). See also, Ball, 1968, 68–70, 73, 316–17. Ball has excellent information on the film, but could not find a print to view in 1968 (90 per cent of Thanhouser product was destroyed by fire in 1917).

[80] Winthrop Ames, New Theatre, New York 28 March 1910. See Bartholomeusz, 1982, 132–40. Thanhhouser's studio in New Rochelle would have been only 45 minutes from Broadway.

The set for Leontes' court is a much-simplified version of Charles Kean's and Mary Anderson's versions of antiquity, including an Alma-Tadema-influenced marble terrace with a view of the Mediterranean. This set and the costumes may well have come from the stock of Thanhouser's previous theatre company. Leontes' few courtiers (as many as the set has room for) wear Roman tunics and sandals, or unidentified exotic robes and headgear. Hermione's ladies wear a mix of styles, including diaphanous ensembles that are part Orientalist painting, part D.W. Griffith biblical epic, but with one lady-in-waiting in a Renaissance dress. Paulina wears a costume with rows of ruffles in the skirt, possibly formed by layers of tunics and a top resembling a brassiere, all of which vaguely resembles an ancient Minoan statue or a Tanagra.

Thanhouser's adaptation is an intelligible version of the play, with side stories and characters (including Mamillius, Time, and the bear) omitted for speed and clarity. The statue scene is missing from the DVD, because the available celluloid copy had lost its final frames. There are invented scenes including one set in prison, where Hermione and her ladies prepare the baby for Paulina to present to Leontes. There is no sense of tragedy, only maternal tenderness as she showers the baby (whose face is not seen) with kisses. A second invented scene is inserted after the trial, reassuringly showing Hermione alive and with Paulina. The intertitle cards are intelligently devised and the easily read descriptions keep to the basic plot: jealous husband, a pregnant wife falsely accused of adultery, imprisonment, banished infant, forbidden young lovers, a prince and a shepherd's daughter who is actually the banished royal baby, a recognition scene, a reunion and a happy ending. It evinced 'unusual enthusiasm' for its time.[81] A *Moving Picture World* review, titled 'Thanhouser Triumph', called it a 'masterpiece' and praised its 'magnificence of mounting, costumes, and the like of which Mr. Thanhouser has taken full advantage'.[82]

Modernism: Lillah McCarthy 1912

In her 1933 memoir, *Myself and My Friends,* Lillah McCarthy (1875–1960) describes how between 1912 and 1914 she shared the management of two

---

[81] Ball, 1968, 69. [82] *Moving Pictures* quoted in Ball, 69.

theatres, and appeared in a production at a third, the Savoy, London, where she worked with her long-time theatre colleague and husband (from 1906 to 1918) Harley Granville-Barker (1877–1946) on his revolutionary productions of *The Winter's Tale* and *Twelfth Night* (she played Hermione and Viola). She writes that the Shakespeare season at the Savoy 'brought me the happiest experience which an actress can have: the playing in company with a splendid cast and enthusiasm of those whose judgement is as sure as it is generous'.[83] The latter may be her veiled reference to Granville-Barker, who had issued an injunction forbidding her to make any reference whatsoever in her memoir to him or his production associates, threatening legal action if she did. This was a major challenge considering how deeply their careers had been intertwined and the importance of that shared work, which included innovative Shakespeare productions and early involvement with George Bernard Shaw's plays.

Among the many pleasures of the memoir is watching McCarthy skilfully negotiate the well-known stories of Granville-Barker's productions with information that shifts the focus away from the 'genius playwright, actor, producer', to include other people involved in the productions. McCarthy praises designers Albert Rutherston[84] (costumes) and Norman Wilkinson (sets) who 'never did finer work than in designing costumes and scenery' for *The Winter's Tale*. She notes in connection to the production, that 'There were many changes from the star-actor-manager's way of producing Shakespeare'. This refers to the streamlined single set and thrust stage introduced with this production, but perhaps also to Granville-Barker himself. When she writes of her conversations with Rutherston on the costumes, it suggests her influence on him to change Granville-Barker's design plans described in his 'Prefaces'. The producer planned costumes that would be Renaissance-classic 'as Shakespeare saw it' and considered the designer in complete agreement, especially after they had 'looked up the artist Giulio Romano' and 'there the costumes were

---

[83] McCarthy, 1933, 156–58.

[84] The designer Albert Rothenstein changed his name to Rutherston during the war; Granville-Barker writing in 1912 refers to him as Rothenstein, the name used for this production; McCarthy in 1933 uses the changed one.

much as we had forethought them'.[85] This is not at all what the actual, costumes looked like. J. L. Styan sums them up as 'Headgear flaunted preposterous plumes, legs were bare with gold and silver boots, dress was boldly embroidered and bespangled'.[86] Instead of 'Renaissance classic' they showed the strong influence of Leon Bakst's costume designs for Sergei Diaghilev's Ballets Russes company, particularly their *Scheherazade* (1911). The costumes were among the production's heavily debated innovations. This modernist *Winter's Tale* had a virtually uncut text and a simple white set, designed by Wilkinson, featuring a backdrop of arches hung with gold, damask curtained and a bare stage with low platform at the back with five steps down. This was used for all scenes and simple changes in props identified new locations. The *Spectator* had reservations about the verse speaking, but applauded this elimination of lengthy scene changes, saying that Granville-Barker 'has shown that an Elizabethan play can be acted without cuts in three hours' and called it 'the most interesting Shakespeare revival that has been seen within the memory of this generation'.[87] There were objections to incompatibility between Rothenstein's costumes and Wilkinson's more austere set. The designer's choice of strong colours also continued the late-Victorian love of bright shades available through aniline dyes from the 1860s onward. The *Westminster Gazette* (23 September 1912) praised the way the white set formed 'a delightful background for the costumes [. . . .] One had a kind of complicated poem of moving colour of a depth greater than that of precious stones'.[88] The fantasy created by this exoticism brings to mind fancy dress parties with *Arabian Nights* themes, made popular at the time by Paul Poiret's 'One Thousand and Second Night' fete in 1911.[89]

One traditional element remained: Hermione was heavily pregnant when she entered upstage centre in 1.2 and walked down the steps followed

---

[85] Granville-Barker, 'Preface', 1912, 24. He does not mention that Romano is referred to in the play, 5.2.95.
[86] See Styan, 1977, 82, 87; Scheijen, 2010, 221, Kennedy, 1985, 123–36.
[87] *Spectator*, September 28, 1912. [88] quoted in Bartholomeusz, 1982, 145–46.
[89] See Poiret, 1931, 98–103.

by a servant, in a feathered turban, who held a silken parasol trimmed with tassels over her head.

In contrast to the brightly coloured costumes of the court and its courtiers, Hermione's costume was a simple variation of antique dress in white or cream. In Figure 2, the *Daily Mirror* Studios photograph, a full-length studio portrait, emphasizes the simplicity of the dress and accessories. The bulky shape of her pregnancy is highlighted by a sash that drapes down from the hips to outline the outer edges of the belly. Like the other costumes, it was from no geographical place, nor historical time. Its lines are reminiscent of Byzantium or Assyrian drawings seen in Walter Crane's and Edmund Dulac's book illustrations.[90] It included a light silk mantle (or shawl) that when she entered was arranged hanging down over her arms, increasing the resemblance to a Poiret robe. Hermione had only one other costume, worn in the third act trial scene, a hooded cape over a loose smock. According to the production photographs, Hermione wore the pregnancy dress again as her statue costume in the fifth act. This is unique, but possibly an aspect of breaking away from the overloaded details of Kean's and Anderson's, spectacular productions. It does present a small conflict with Shakespeare's text because when Leontes exclaims: 'O, thus she stood, / Even with such majesty – warm life, / As now it coldly stands – ', he also says she looks as 'when I first wooed her' (5.3.34-36). Since this is an experimental and revolutionary production, would that detail of when he first saw her justify the cost and fuss of the third costume?

Figure 2 shows the actress as George Bernard Shaw has described her: 'She was beautiful, plastic, statuesque, most handsome made, and seemed to have come straight from the Italian or eighteenth-century stage without a trace of the stuffiness of the London cup-and-saucer theatres'.

McCarthy may have been the first modern Hermione, rejecting earlier sentimentality and bringing to the role a strong flavour of the Shavian 'New Woman'. Shaw had wanted to find another Sarah Siddons to play his

---

[90] The frontispiece in *Myself and My Friends* is Dulac's drawing of McCarthy dressed in ancient style. Jacques Copeau's 1920 costume design for Hermione also uses similar design.

Performing Visible Pregnancy in Shakespeare's Plays 39

Figure 2 Visible Pregnancy 1912. Lillah McCarthy (Hermione) in costume for scenes 1.2, 2.1 and 5.3, director Harley Granville-Barker, designer Albert Rutherston. Image courtesy of Shakespeare Birthplace Trust.

women, and felt he had found her with McCarthy. He could have been describing Hermione when he wrote: 'The horrible artificiality of that impudent sham the Victorian womanly woman, a sham manufactured by men for men, and duly provided by the same for the same with a bulbously overclothed "modesty" more lascivious than any frank sensuality.'[91]

---

[91] Shaw, 1933, 5, 8.

Disappearing Visibility: Disappearing Pregnancy 1931–1960

McCarthy was the last of the significantly visibly pregnant Hermione until past the middle of the twentieth century. The following decades saw visible pregnancy melt away into near invisibility.

Productions at the Shakespeare Festival Theatre between 1931 and 1960 are representative of the decline in a visible pregnancy. In 1931 Dorothy Massingham (Hermione) in W. Bridges Adams' regal and formal production did have a pregnancy curve in her simple medieval costume.[92] In the single available photograph (by Claude Harris, Regent Street, London) she draws attention to her pregnant shape by resting an elegant hand just above the nicely rounded, discreet bump. In Anthony Quayle's 1948 production the sets and costumes were designed by Motley (Margaret Harris, Sophia Harris, and Elizabeth Montgomery) who chose a Russian milieu that was part Bakst, and part illustrated Russian fairy tale. *The Times* thought the Sicilian scene's 'Asiatic setting is not only strange and beautiful itself but the strangeness suits' the tale (7 June 1948). The *Manchester Guardian* complained that the spectacle of Sicilia made Bohemia look dull in comparison (7 June 1948). Photographs show Diana Wynyard as a young and less formal queen, with little or no pregnancy shape. She is shown with Mamillius on her lap, laughing and hugging him so closely to her chest that there would not have been room for a pregnancy prosthesis. She would be similarly flat-ish bellied in Peter Brook's 1951 production.

The ultimate lack of visible pregnancy was Elizabeth Sellars' costume in 1960. As seen in Figure 3, there is a once-upon-a-time fairy tale quality to her tall gold crown and the dress. The photograph shows an unornamented dark coloured Elizabethan-ish bodice worn over a gathered skirt in a lighter colour and fabric, and a diaphanous cloak that rests lightly on her shoulders. The bodice skims the torso, emphasizes the slim waist where it stops, but in front continues over her stomach in a smooth and faintly curved V shape. Even the slight indication of pregnancy seen in Jacques Noël's original design has disappeared.[93] As with Brook's earlier production, the convention of visible

---

[92] Production programme, 1931, *The Winter's Tale*, SBT Collections.

[93] The designer's drawing is included in the SBT blog: 'Shakespeare-by-Design =Pretty+Important' by Robyn Greenwood, 14 August '2013', available at Shakespeare.org.uk.

Figure 3 No Visible Pregnancy 1960. Elizabeth Sellars (Hermione), director Peter Wood, designer Jacques Noël. Photo: Angus McBean ©Houghton Library, Harvard University

pregnancy had been quietly diminished and then dropped in line with a societal construction that bracketed off the presence of pregnant women. It was rare to see a major character in either classic or modern dramas appear pregnant. When they did they were usually lower class, as in Shelagh Delaney's *A Taste of Honey* (1959, film 1961) and Tennessee Williams' *A Streetcar Named Desire* (1947, film 1961). A notable exception is the very pregnant young wife of a sailor, in a respectable working class family, in Noël Coward's film *In Which We Serve* (1945), but she is a minor character. Television, broadcast into the home, was thought to require careful scrutiny and censorship about language pertaining to pregnancy. The weekly half-hour comedy *I Love Lucy* (1951–1957) on American television was the unique example that overcame prudery and incorporated the actress Lucille Ball's actual pregnancy (1952) into the character. Ball was chief investor and producer, as well as the star of the very popular series. Her position was powerful enough to challenge the CBS network's decision to cancel the programme when it learned of her pregnancy. With the commercial sponsor's support, she insisted on the show continuing and the result was even higher ratings. But she did wear the smock[94] and the word 'pregnant' was never used. The pregnancy was announced in the press as Ball being 'enceinte'.[95]

Peter Brook 1951

The most important mid-century version of *The Winter's Tale* was Peter Brook's 1951 production at the Phoenix Theatre, the Tennents/Arts Council entry in the Festival of Britain. The cast featured well-known actors: John Gielgud (Leontes), Diana Wynyard (Hermione), Flora Robson (Paulina). Brook created a scaled down bare-stage production with a thrust stage and modified Elizabethan costumes, designed by Sophie Fedorovitch, a designer noted for her 'method of scrupulous elimination'.[96] In this production that included eliminating visible pregnancy. The costume seen in Figure 4 is notable for its minimal gesture towards Hermione's pregnancy. The production was well received by critics, popular with audiences and, unexpectedly, one of the festival's most successful offerings; it set a record for a *Winter's*

---

[94] From the 1940s onward standard maternity wear included a hip-length smock; previously women had let out pleats, layered garments, or hitched the dress up over the belly, preferably letting out the hem to keep it level.

[95] The confrontation was the subject of the bio-pic *Being the Ricardos*, 2021, dir. Aaron Sorkin, Nicole Kidman as Ball. The one episode in the TV series where the very pregnant Ball did not wear the smock was when she disguised herself as an older man with a very large belly in order to sneak into a men's only party.

[96] Kavanagh, 31. The earliest example of Brook's move to simplified sets and costumes was his cancellation of an elaborate set for *Romeo and Juliet* in Stratford upon Avon in 1947, just days before the opening; the play took place on an empty stage.

Performing Visible Pregnancy in Shakespeare's Plays 43

Figure 4 Disappearing Pregnancy 1951. Brewster Mason (Polixenes), Diana Wynyard (Hermione), in background, John Gielgud (Leontes), director Peter Brook, designer Sophie Fedorovitch. Photo: Angus McBean ©Houghton Library, Harvard University

Tale theatrical run, topping Mary Anderson's record of 164 performances with its 167. The *Sunday Express* called it 'magnificent Shakespeare' (1 July 1951). *Theatre World Annual 1952* praised the 'delightful production' and thought its 'cast-iron box office success [was a] splendid example of Shakespeare's evergreen appeal to the man in the street of every generation'. *The Times* reviewer found the 'graceful, measured production, wholly free from personal caprice' (which Brook was noted for) and praised Brook and the company for being 'careful to veil the characters from too searching a psychology' (28 June 1951). Michael Kustow quotes Ivor Brown's comment in the *Observer* that it 'leaves out Peter Brookishness and is admirably simple and quick'.[97] According to J. C. Trewin: 'For years there had not been in London a less ostentatious production of Shakespeare.'[98]

Wynyard's Hermione was 'magnificent' (*Daily Express* 28 June 1951) and 'coolly statuesque even before her translation in delicate pink draperies – a vision not to be forgotten'.[99] Her 1948 performance of Hermione at the Shakespeare Memorial Theatre, directed by Anthony Quayle, had received similar enthusiastic reviews.

Fedorovitch's costumes were rich but sombre for Sicilia, which in Angus McBean's photographs appears only as a dark background. Wynyard's blonde hair and fair skin are the two surfaces that catch the light in most of these pictures. Figure 4, where Polixenes kneels before Hermione who playfully holds a toy dagger to his heart, is an exception. His embroidered doublet is light coloured, and also establishes the Elizabethan period more clearly than Hermione's generic costume does. Its main signifier of the period is the small stand-up lace collar (a rebato) at the back of the neckline. The regal Wynyard wears a dark velvet dress with a close-fitting bodice, tight sleeves, a slender waist, and a belt that crosses horizontally across her flattish abdomen. It is a hybrid that both has and has not a visible pregnancy. Under the dress a roll of padding is placed around the hips allowing the skirt to drape slightly outward, but evenly, and with no evident pregnancy. Even this bit of bulk is not always visible in reproductions of the image because the area is shadowed. It also disappears when the printed photo is cropped just below the waist. The costume reflects the 1950s prudish social conventions regarding visible pregnancy, but more influential was Brook's own agenda. Given the conventions of the times, it may not have occurred to him or Fedorovitch to shape Hermione realistically. It is possible that Brook was simply not interested in the size of a pregnant belly, and indifferent to the way it could affect a performance. He used a similar Elizabethan-style costume with no sign of pregnancy for Juliet's first appearance in *Measure for Measure*.[100]

---

[97] Kustow, 2005, 69.   [98] Trewin, 1971, 19.
[99] *Theatre World Annual (London) Number 3*. 1952. Rockcliff, 36–40. (36).
[100] See Styan, 1977, Plate 23.

His staging experiment with *The Winter's Tale* introduced the stripped-down style that would come to define his work as a director/producer. The costume choices are conventional Shakespearean. Non-visible pregnancy may be Brook's deliberate choice, an element in his mix of conforming and not conforming with convention.[101] Writing in *Vogue* Siriol Hugh-Jones summed up the production's effect: 'Having delighted, ravished and infuriated us in former productions with fabulous crowd skirmishing, shock effects, thistledown elegancies of style, and occasionally bloody-minded naughtiness, he now straightens his box of bricks into neat piles to build scaffolding for the play, and nothing but the play.'[102] Omitting visible pregnancy may be part of the neat pattern, and certainly no one objected to the glamourous trim-waisted Hermione. However, a few years later there were two North American productions where visible pregnancy was glamourous, even if unnoticed. In the 1950s and 1960s pregnancy was still dealt with discreetly, not a topic for public conversation, or as some would argue, even for public presentation. Prohibitions and inhibitions were beginning to change, especially when the feminist movement brought the female body into political discourse. The two designs that reintroduced visible pregnancy were early signs that the social thaw that had been coming slowly, was now on the horizon.

A Glimpse of Visible Pregnancy: Stratford, Ontario 1958, NYC 1963

The two North American productions of *The Winter's Tale* were the Stratford Festival, Ontario in 1958 (designed by Tanya Moisiewitch, directed by Donald Campbell) and the New York Shakespeare Festival in New York City in 1963 (designed by Theoni V. Aldredge, directed by Gladys Vaughn). Both were summer Shakespeare festivals. Stratford Ontario's began in 1952, opened its permanent theatre in 1957, and was the more established of the two. New York City's festival was the work of Joe Papp, founder of the off-Broadway Public Theater. Papp, committed to bringing free outdoor summer Shakespeare to the city, opened the

---

[101] J. C. Trewin in *Peter Brook: A Biography*. 1971, 19.

[102] quoted by J. C. Trewin, 1971, 59.

Delacorte Theater in Central Park in 1962. For both companies this was their second season in their own theatres and their first production of *The Winter's Tale*. In 1963 a third summer festival in Stratford, Connecticut also included the play, but there seems to be no accessible record of Hermione's costumes.

Tracking costumes with visible pregnancies through photographs is not always reliable. For example, there are two photographs in the Ontario Festival's archives of the 1958 Hermione (Charmion King) in 1.2. Her costume, a sumptuous collation of fabrics and jewels, included a visible pregnancy, but in the image where the queen sits the pregnancy is not visible. In the other image, where she stands, the pregnancy is large and emphasized by Hermione's left arm curved under the belly, barely touching it, while her right arm rested just above it. The pose for this photo, which was used for publicity, is reminiscent of seventeenth-century pregnancy portraits, including some of Van Dyck's paintings of Henrietta Maria.[103] Dennis Behl, working with the festival's costume bible, describes Hermione's dress for 1.2 as 'tangerine-shot taffeta with sleeves appliqued in gold, pearls, and studs. White marquisette was used at the neck and sleeve; a pale pink and yellow-shot organza drape completed the costume'. She also wore a tiara, had jewels intertwined in her hair, a necklace hooked to the bodice, shoulder broches, rings, and golden slippers. He notes that 'Padding indicated her pregnancy'.[104] For 2.1, the nursery scene, the court robes were removed, and replaced by a blue velvet robe with brown fur trim over a blue underrobe. In the trial scene the costume drawing shows her with her hands chained behind her back; the costume is a duplicate of the underrobe, now stained and distressed, the pregnancy padding removed. Her diminished splendour included a veil of pale grey silk jersey hung from her hair; a length of mushroom-coloured tricot hung from her shoulders.[105]

All of the production's costumes were elaborate and placed the play in an eclectic, lush mix of periods.[106] The staging irritated the *New York Times* critic Brooks Atkinson who objected to Campbell's 'emphasis on seeing – on

---

[103] See National Portrait Gallery website, *Henrietta Maria* by Van Dyck.
[104] Behl, 1994, 93. [105] Edelstein, 1994, Plate 30 *Hermione*.
[106] Behl, 1994, 91–98. (92); Edelstein, 1994, see Plate 29 *Camillo*.

spectacular processions with flambeaux, big court scenes with many attendants [. . .] stunning costumes, ornate properties' that placed the visual over dramatic interpretation and made 'the innocent play of *The Winter's Tale* almost an afterthought' (22 July 1958). In the *Shakespeare Quarterly* Arnold Edinborough complained that the director had missed the serious symbolism of the play and left it a confusing 'rag bag of a play'.[107]

Five years later another fully pregnant Hermione appeared on stage when *The Winter's Tale,* directed by Gladys Vaughan, was included in New York Shakespeare Theater's 1963 season in Central Park. The *New York Times'* review included a photograph of Salome Jens (Hermione) in a simple medieval/Renaissance dress with a clearly defined pregnancy curve. The play would have been unknown to many in the socially mixed New York audience. British theatrical conventions were irrelevant here, and a visibly pregnant Hermione was as crucial for this audience to follow the story as it had been for Tanhouser's film. The costume was simple, undecorated, and had a mixed medieval and Renaissance silhouette that was slim on the body except where it was rounded out by the pregnancy. The neckline was discretely scooped; the sleeves tight and the fabric heavy enough to flow smoothly over the belly. The fabric looks rich, but, considering the company's limited budget, it was probably purchased at bargain prices in the city's garment district. Alice Griffin in *Shakespeare Quarterly* complained about the distracting lack of an overall design style which made her feel this 'could only have been inspired by a turn-of-the-century production where each costume was [as] opulent and striking as possible, without stressing character and mood'.[108] But questions of costumes and historic periods were a frequent complaint in reviews during the second half of the twentieth century. Some reviewers still longed for the ancient world as the correct setting for this play, while others objected to eclectic mixes, or wanted more of the fable/fairy tale quality. By the end of the century a comfortable mid-Victorian or Romanov period had become one of the most popular settings, as seen in Gregory Doran's version in 1999 and Kenneth Branagh's in 2015. It became nearly as standard for

---

[107] Edinbrough, 1958, *Shakespeare Quarterly*, vol 9 issue 4, 531.
[108] Griffin, 1963, *Shakespeare Quarterly*, vol 14, 442.

productions as the classical world had been. Among its merits was the fashionable accommodation of large pregnancies in beautiful dresses.

Visibility Returns: Judi Dench, Trevor Nunn, RSC 1969

Trevor Nunn's RSC production of *The Winter's Tale* in 1969 was a breakthrough in many ways: sets, lights, verse speaking, contemporary values, absence of pomp and ceremony. The youthfulness of the royals as a modern family was a major theme. When the stage lights came up Leontes, Hermione and Polixenes entered laughing, and playing tag with Mamillius.[109] Hermione and Perdita were doubled for the first time since Mary Anderson in 1887, and Hermione's costume included a very pronounced visible pregnancy, possibly for the first time in four decades in the United Kingdom. Ronald Bryden summed up the family's domesticity: 'The young father kindles with pride in his small son. His wife, the shape of a coming child swelling her white gown, glows like a pearl with contentment as she watches them play' (*Observer* 18 May 1969).

This time the inclusion of an accurately sized pregnancy silhouette had a wide-reaching and permanent impact. It was the turning point after which, with minor variations, this became the consistent practice for Hermione's costume in 1.2 and 2.1, no matter what the setting or the period. The thin pregnancy cushion disappeared without anyone noticing, and it has not returned. Here, as seen throughout this brief history, the visible pregnancy of Hermione coincided with, or was subtly directed by, cultural and social attitudes. This included a loosening of social prohibitions, altered conventions of propriety, the 'sexual revolution'. The clothes-shedding musical *Hair* proclaimed it the 'Age of Aquarius'. The law in the UK ended homosexuality's illegality and abolished theatre censorship, including the ban on nudity.[110] The emergence of

---

[109] The promptbook meticulously lists who touches whom: Mamillius is 'it'; he touches Polixenes who touches Mamillius who touches Leontes who goes to touch Polixenes. The action takes place around a large toy box and large rocking horse.

[110] This allowed on stage nudity in *Hair*, Gerome Ragni and James Rado's musical, New York, April 1968, imported to London's Shaftesbury Theatre

'youth culture' in the 1960s created a revolution in fashion. A creative mix of invention and retro emerged that both inspired and changed the way many young people dressed. Rock stars set the style, but so did clothing by young British designers including: Mary Quant, modern crisp, cheap and mini-skirted; Laura Ashley, Edwardian romantic, long and flowing; and Vivienne Westwood, fancy Teddy Boys evolving into grunge. Freedom of choice was the guideline, and this was the way director Trevor Nunn and designer Christopher Morley, both in their twenties, dressed *The Winter's Tale*. Sicilia's young royals could have been playing dress-up in inherited Regency clothing just as London's young aristocrats were doing with finds from ancestral trunks in the attic. The costumes were an unexpected version of counter-culture dress.

Trevor Nunn used the production to make a bold statement of the direction he wanted the company to follow. He replaced Peter Hall's political focus with one that paid greater attention to the play's social and familial aspects, all to be done with the simplest of sets, and with a resident group of actors. It was the beginning of an era in the theatre where it became 'easier to recall directors rather the actors'.[111] The production was 'the most significant and effective embodiment' of the director's commitment to 'modernity and seriousness [....] capturing the spirit of the times while reasserting the play's centrality in the canon'.[112] Innovations included replacing the courtiers' opening scene with the disembodied voice of Time; casting the same actress for Hermione and Perdita; staging the sheep shearing as a hippie Be-In; making Time a man in a plexiglass box illuminated by strobe lights; and dimming lights so the audience saw what Leontes imagined. The music was Indian sitars in Sicilia and rock in Bohemia. Critical reception of Nunn's experiment was mixed, as might be expected. Typical of positive reviews of the emphasis on youth was Gareth

September 1968, ran for 1,997 performances and *O Calcutta*, devised by Kenneth Tynan, New York, Off Broadway 1969, London's West End, 1970 3,900 performances.

[111] Evans, 1970, 132, 133. He listed directors: Trevor Nunn, John Barton, Terry Hands, and Peter Brook.

[112] Jackson, 2019, 44–53 (45).

Lloyd Evans in the *Guardian* who welcomed 'the near-miracle of illuminating and preserving Shakespeare's text with a thoroughly contemporary interpretation' (17 May 1969). John Barber praised 'the impact of reality [that] was lent to the situation by setting the opening scene in the Palace nursery' (*Telegraph* 17 May 1969). In the *Daily Express*, Herbert Kretzmer applauded it as 'a magical production' (16 May 1969). Less enthusiastic critics disliked the 'bland'/'sterile'/'antiseptic'/stark white tiled box set and objected that Nunn 'got carried away by his visual gimmicks'. J. C. Trewin in the *Birmingham Post* complained about the omission of the opening scene, the lights, the set, and the 'irritating costumes' (18 May 1969).

This was the year before the first Glastonbury Festival, and Morley's designs for dress in Bohemia were hippie-inspired. Barefoot and long-haired the shepherds had 'Red Indian headbands and bare midriffs' (J. W. Lambert, *The Times* 18 May 1969). The even longer-haired shepherdesses mixed brightly coloured sarongs, skimpy tops, and miniskirts with hippie flair.

Reviewers found Sicilia's all-white clothing more challenging to identify with a specific historical period. The setting was a bare stage in a white box, but the whiteness of its props – even the large rocking horse – and costumes (seen in Figure 5) implied modernity. For Patricia E. Tatspaugh, the 'whiteness of set, properties (and programme) and the pseudo-Regency costumes suggested innocence, purity and winter'.[113] There was, however, one note of colour. In black-and-white photographs of the scene it is easy to miss that Polixenes wore a red jacket. It linked him to the colours in Bohemia, but also identified him as the outsider in this family group. The royals' retro-Regency costumes puzzled some writers as to historical nomenclature: Leontes' court was said to be dressed in 'Kate Greenaway clothes' (Philip Hope-Wallace, *Guardian*, 3 July 1970) and, more accurately, the men were described dressed as 'Regency beaux' (*Sunday Telegraph* 18 May 1969). Hilary Spurling in the *Spectator* thought that everything, including the men's ruffled shirts, flared jackets and high-waisted trousers ... suggests the youth, wealth and arrogance of the Sicilian court' (23 May 1969). The clearest identification of the director's and designer's purpose is Martin Esslin's review in the *New York Times*:

---

[113] Tatspaugh, 2002, 33–39 (35). Spearling is quoted by Tatspaugh, 36.

Performing Visible Pregnancy in Shakespeare's Plays 51

Figure 5 Visible Pregnancy Returns 1969, costumes for Acts 1 and 2, Barrie Ingham (Leontes), Judi Dench (Hermione), Richard Pasco (Polixenes), director Trevor Nunn, designer Christopher Morley. Photo: Reg Wilson ©RSC

> The costumes are a strange mixture, which help make the play both part of a romantic epoch of Regency and Carnaby Street into which the strange fairy tale of jealousy and love fits extremely well, and wholly contemporary. Carnaby Street is very much like the Regency style. We get the best of both worlds. (1 June 1969)

It was essential for the successful doubling that Hermione and Perdita should appear as different from each other as possible.[114] Learning about Mary Anderson's production had suggested the doubling to Nunn. Dench's Hermione and Perdita were complete opposites in hair, dress, posture, attitude, movement, and accent. Hermione's Regency style is elegant, witty but controlled, her expression serene. The visible pregnancy defined her. Her dress was undecorated, smooth-surfaced without frills, with long sleeves that hugged the arm and a discreetly curved neckline without lace, ruffles, or other trim. Designed in the manner of Regency fashion it had a simple gathering under the bust from which the body of the dress sloped smoothly down to the floor to form a modest circle that widened into the merest hint of a train around the back. Figure 5 shows that the well-developed pregnancy seemed especially present when she sat and the dress's fabric draped toward the side, forming a soft deep fold on either side of the belly, drawing the eye to its roundness.[115] Gareth Lloyd Evans' *Guardian* review is representative of critical acclaim for the casting: 'Judi Dench's doubling as Perdita and Hermione achieves, especially as the latter, a presence which touches greatness' (17 May 1969).

The RSC and SBT Collections confirm that the original costume no longer exists, and there is no known copy of the costume bible and no accessible video of the performance. There is, however, the promptbook and an extensive collection of photographs give a valuable picture of how the dress worked in performance. These include works by an unusually long list of photographers for an RSC production.[116] Most of the pictures feature the rocking horse, the

---

[114] The substitution in the statue scene used a familiar bit of staging – the group, including Perdita, walked around the statue's curtained dais. When they were out of sight, Dench changed places with a replacement Perdita. When the group came to stand in front of the dais, the curtain was drawn to reveal Dench as the statue.

[115] See Davidson, 2023, *Jane Austen's Closet* for examples of Regency style, esp. Danish wedding dress, 1.4.

[116] Photographers included Joe Cocks, Malcom Davies, Jonathan Docker-Drysdale, Zuleika Henry, Tim Holt, Angus McBean, and Reg Wilson. RSC *Winter's Tale* promptbook, photo boxes and envelopes, SBT Collection.

white boxes that served as seats and a toy box, Leontes, Polixenes, and at the centre Dench's Hermione, radiantly content and very visibly pregnant. In Bohemia Dench's teenage Perdita was all Botticelli billowing dress and flowing long hair. That was the striking image used for posters. But black-and-white versions set in the nursery were the primary ones used in publicity images at the time and remain the standard illustrations of, among Nunn's many new devices, a highly emphasized presence of Hermione's pregnancy.[117]

Sometimes a costume's history has its own narrative. If there is a romance to that history, as Barbara Hodgdon claims can happen, then this 1969 costume, imagined by Trevor Nunn, designed by Christopher Morley, worn by Judi Dench, has just such a story.[118] Drawing on a dress someone had seen and remembered for eighteen years is the stuff of the theatre's romance.

Judi Dench Remembers:

> It was Trevor's production, as you know, designed by Chris Morley, and I can remember Trevor saying that he had seen Leslie Caron arriving at the theatre, when she was married to Peter [Hall] of course, very pregnant in a white dress. I remember very early on he said that and Chris Morley and he talked about it and that's why we did that. But that's how it originated. It was Trevor seeing Leslie going into the theatre once in a white dress and being very pregnant.[119]

5 When Pregnancy Is Visible: What Actors Say about Performing Hermione's Pregnancy

Images projected on stage tell us what to think about the woman in the play. And about women in the audiences.

Fiona Shaw, in Rutter, 1988, xxii[120]

---

[117] SBT production photographs for 1969, and RSC-held photographs.
[118] See Hodgdon (2006) on Peggy Ashcroft's cardigan, 160.
[119] Recorded voice mail sent privately to me. [120] See Rutter, 1988, Intoduction

Nineteenth-century actresses were considered to 'own' certain Shakespeare roles, which they toured with for years and even decades. Twentieth- and twenty-first-century female actors also own parts, but in a different way. They may play Hermione in only one production during their career, but that performance remains an accessible part of the play's performance history. This is true for performances of Hermione by Gemma Jones, Alexandra Gilbreath, and Kelly Hunter who have written and spoken about their experiences with the role. Important for this study is the attention they pay to negotiating the impact of Hermione's pregnancy on the character and their physical experience of working with a pregnancy prosthesis.[121] All three were in Royal Shakespeare Company productions. If a nineteenth- or early twentieth-century actress spoke about Hermione's pregnancy, it would be in veiled references as with Helen Faucit's thoughts about the 'trial to come'. Contemporary actresses, on the other hand, speak openly about Hermione's pregnancy, as well as their own.

After Nunn's production, Hermione's realistic, highly visible pregnancy became an unquestioned theatrical convention. In the RSC productions between 1976 and 2009, having the pregnant belly visible and touchable meant that it received specific attention in physical encounters. It worked almost as a prop that encouraged experimentation in the interactions of Leontes, Polixenes, Mamillius, and Hermione. Details of performances have been reconstructed for this study through archival and commercial recordings, costume bibles, and the stage managers' promptbooks. This section adds the actresses' own memories about working within the framework of Hermione's visible pregnancy. Their conversations help explain why everyone on stage in their productions seems conscious of the unborn baby, especially Leontes' and Polixenes' physical relationship to Hermione's body. Jones, Gilbreath, and Hunter had never acted in pregnancy costume before, nor had they realized the limits the inanimate prosthesis placed on body movement. Perhaps because they strapped on the pregnancy shape for only a short time each day, it seemed more restrictive than an actual pregnancy. For each of them Hermione became

---

[121] Rutter, 1988, xii

a personal negotiation with the costume and the character. Their own voices below are an important part of the archives.

Gemma Jones played Hermione in 1981–1983 in Stratford-upon-Avon, London and on tour in Japan. The production was directed by Ronald Eyre, with Patrick Stewart as Leontes and Ray Jewers as Polixenes. The set was basically a raised platform, an empty thrust stage with the audience seated on three sides. The magic was in the costumes designed by Chris Dyer. They counter-balanced any austerity of the setting. Seen in photographs and in the RSC's archival recording (over-lit and distanced by the use of a single camera), they suggest a non-specific world that is part fairy tale. Ella Hawkins classifies their period style as 'Abstract/eclectic', a design that is 'partially stylized' but unlike 'any period of dress history' and with 'blended styles from multiple time periods'.[122]

The production opened with a masque with the royals in impressionistically seventeenth-/eighteenth-century dress, in the manner of Edmund Dulac's illustrations for Perrault's courtly fairy tales.[123]

Jones described her costumes for the masque, where she is the 'fanciful' queen, as pale, soft, light and lovely'.[124] Her dress, seen in Figure 6, is a wide-sleeved over-mantle (Dyer's term), with gathering under the bust that increases the pregnancy's visibility. The semi-transparent fabric is decorated with painted blobs suggesting the shapes of abstract flowers in blue, red, yellow. On the fabric swatch attached by straight pin to the costume drawing, the colours are more vibrant than expected, and each 'blob' is outlined with an embroidered, chainstitched, narrow gold thread. A long blonde wig with a coronet of flowers was designed to cover the actress' own hair which had been cropped for the trial scene.

In Dyer's pencil sketches on large sheets of watercolour paper, the costumes for Sicilia are undecorated garments of great simplicity. Hermione and Paulina both wear sleek, long robes that skim down the body to the floor and button down the front; the sleeves are slender but not tight and there is a small mandarin collar close to the neck. The garments

---

[122] Hawkins, 2022, 194.
[123] See *Perrault's Fairy Tales Illustrated by Edmund Dulac*. Folio Society, 2000.
[124] Jones, 2000, 158.

Figure 6 1981 After the masque, scene in 1.2. Ray Jewers (Polixenes) Gemma Jones (Hermione) Patrick Stewart (Leontes): director Ronald Eyre; designer Chris Dyer. Photo Reg Wilson ©RSC

manage to look both exotic and as simple as cassocks. Swatches of the fabrics used for the first two acts' elegant costumes are in a mix of fabrics and textures in shades of white, ivory, cream, and ecru. Dyer's design sketches include notes that clarify but also add subtle indications of his attitude towards the project. The information on the sketch for 2.1, set in the privacy of the nursery, specifies she has taken off the masque costume that had been worn over this garment. He titled the sketch for that first dress 'Masque'; the second design for 2.1, the nursery scene, is (rather charmingly) titled 'Domestic'. No visible pregnancy is indicated in the drawing, but it is not ignored. Dyer has lightly drawn, in a single line, a rectangle framing the belly, and identified the space as 'pregnancy'. This is unusual. Generally, designers seem reluctant to engage with the pregnancy belly and its dimensions for Hermione's costume. The size and construction of the pregnancy are left to the director and costume shop that will supervise the construction. None of the few existing earlier costume bibles that I have been able to examine in the RSC archives include any instructions or dimensions. For example, Robert Jones' drawings for the 1999 production, set in the late nineteenth century, show dresses for Hermione's pregnancy scenes that are tightly corseted and almost identical with Paulina's.

The actress writes about her experiences with the role and the costume in her *Players of Shakespeare* essay on Hermione. She is frank about her difficulties with finding a way into the role and how her own experience with pregnancy helped. It was extremely challenging coming to grips with what was for her the unbelievable goodness of Hermione and the question of how this 'truly good woman' could be so unaware of what is happening to her husband. Finally, she wrote a note to herself on her script: 'think pregnant'. She thought about the sense of satisfaction she felt at the time of her own pregnancy. She became hyperaware of pregnancy in others. She remembered looking out the bus window on the way home from rehearsal and thinking, 'North London seems to be populated with pregnant women: I wonder that we can feel so unique and miraculous when there are so many of us'. She was in 'a state of introverted self-satisfaction which allowed for no intrusion and blinded me to needs outside myself'. She explored the effect of pregnancy on relationships in conversations with Patrick Stewart and Ray Jewers. Both were fathers and they 'acknowledged having certain feelings of impotent isolation and rejection'.

Eventually, it no longer seemed strange to her that Hermione was not aware of what was happening to her husband: 'I reasoned that if Hermione is in a state of maternity, this can embrace not only the child that she has [Mamillius] and the child that she carries but also her husband and his childhood friend in an entirely chaste and compassionate love'. Even so, with so much seemingly settled, her costume presented further uncertainty. Usually, actors talk about the familiar pattern of realizing who their character is when they see themselves in full costume for the first time. Gemma Jones had the opposite reaction and writes that when she regards herself 'in my new wig, make-up, padding and costume' the 'tenuous grasp' she has 'upon my role thus far seems to slip further away'. The costume made her worry about: the amount of time for costume changes; whether she could step on and off a platform without 'walking up my dress', even worrying that she would begin to 'look like an American football player' if she added any more body protection than the knee pads needed when she swooned in the trial scene when hearing that Mamillius is dead. On her list padding is separate from costume, so could also be the pregnancy prosthesis in addition to knee pads. When a character is padded out, or corseted in, something similar is worn in rehearsal. She grew quite fond of her pregnancy padding, though she writes that it came in for 'a deal of ribald comment'. Even that ribaldry became part of the experience of acting pregnancy that led to her understanding of Hermione's pure goodness as 'necessary to illuminate the irrationality of Leontes' jealousy'.[125]

Alexandra Gilbreath played Hermione in Gregory Doran's 1999 RSC production with Antony Sher as Leontes. In *Players of Shakespeare 5* she writes about her experience with the play in general, her understanding of Hermione, and how the pregnancy shaped her performance. This included the early scenes in the Sicilian court where Hermione is the glamourous expectant queen, and also her post-natal shattered condition in the trial scene. Discussing Hermione's first two scenes, Gilbreath describes how she worked with her costume's realistic body shape to convey the pregnancy's effects. The setting was a Romanov world at the end of the nineteenth century. Figure 7, where Hermione and Leontes sit pleasantly together, shows the opulence of the fabric and dress and also the dominance of the pregnancy shape. Robert Jones designed costumes that were realistic to the period, but to Gilbreath they were 'rather restricting and formal'.[126] The shape of the pregnancy prosthesis was arranged, as usual, by the costume shop and is not in the designer's drawings in the costume bible. The padding was realistically large and made even larger by the dress's fullness. Gilbreath wanted Hermione to be as 'ripe' and 'female' as possible: 'I wanted her to glow with the expectancy of her unborn child. Motherhood to Hermione is a beautiful thing. Pregnancy suits her; it therefore makes her supremely vulnerable'. She set the pregnancy at eight-and-a-half-months, nearly full term, which she thought made the baby's 'survival in the wilderness as viable as possible'.

---

[125] Jones, 1989, 156, 158, 159. [126] Gilbreath, 2003, 77

Figure 7 Opulent Pregnancy 1999 Scene 1.2 Alexandra Gilbreath (Hermione) Antony Sher (Leontes), Estelle Kohler (Paulina), director Gregory Doran, designer Robert Jones. Photo: Malcolm Davies ©Shakespeare Birthplace Trust

In her writing Gilbreath absorbs Hermione's pregnancy, speaking of it in the first person as though it was her own pregnancy: 'Having never been pregnant before, I took myself off to some pre-natal classes ….' She describes this part of her research causing 'no end of mirth' among the expectant mums as she 'happily' stroked her rehearsal 'bump'. Watching, listening, and considering her own possible pregnant stage movements, she also became aware of the women's 'keen sense of terror and excitement!' From rehearsing wearing the 'bump' she knew the pregnant body's restrictions and realized how much it would tire Hermione and make her impatient with Mamillius at the beginning of 2.1. Pregnancy helped Gilbreath understand Hermione's own unawareness of the effect her gentle flirtatiousness had on Leontes. 'I suppose that what I really wanted to achieve is the sense that she has absolutely no idea what is happening in Leontes' mind, that her flirtatiousness with Polixenes and her teasing of her husband are oblivious of the volatile emotional situation.'[127] To her, Hermione seemed to have, somehow, felt safe in her pregnancy. In the production when Leontes watches Polixenes and Hermione's chaste waltz, his jealousy sees only 'paddling palms', 'pinching fingers' and 'practised smiles / As in a looking glass' (1.2.115-16). But at that moment Gilbreath would imagine that 'the baby moved in my womb, at which I would let out an involuntary gasp, thus prompting his next line "and then to sigh, as 'twere / The mort o'th'deer"' (1.2.117-18). She was deliberately, but gradually, setting the way to the humiliation and shocking violence of the nursery scene (2.1), which ended with Gilbreath's Hermione going into labour.

Antony Sher's Leontes was a man driven to violence by an imagined betrayal. Gilbreath remembers that 'We talked initially about the domestic violence in the play; that essentially it is about a family disintegrating; it just so happens that it's all very public and that the family is of the royal variety'. She describes how when Leontes enters the female world of the nursery and accuses Hermione of treachery, 'it happens with such speed and physical ferocity'. He attacks her verbally and then turns on her with physical violence, throwing her to the floor and pulling at her clothes. Heavily pregnant, she is unable to get up without help. He stands in front of her, but walks away when she holds out her hand for help. Her ladies stand frozen, not moving until Leontes gives the signal. As Hermione is taken away to prison she goes into labour and 'the physical pains of imminent childbirth as a result of his brutal treatment were for all to see'.

In the third act Gilbreath continued to explore the physicality of Hermione's pregnancy through her post-partum appearance at the trial. The actor thought about the ways Leontes would have continued to torment Hermione in prison. The DVD makes it possible to see how this unfolded. As Hermione enters it is clear she has been dragged into court almost directly after giving birth. She was still weak, haggard, slim as a wraith, hair chopped off, dressed in a blood-stained shift, barefoot and manacled. Gilbreath could hear the audience's gasp at every performance

---

[127] Gilbreath, 2003, 75, 77–80, 82.

on this entrance. This is the reaction she wanted. She had made the entrance 'as visually alarming as possible [with] the effects of childbirth still there for all to see, with a huge blood-stain on the back of my dress'. She wondered about how horrid and painful this birth would have been in a dirty rat-infested cell. Was Hermione still experiencing pain? Did she require medical attention? The actor wanted to have 'physical traits to make her as vulnerable as possible, thus highlighting her remarkable strength of character and her ability to endure enormous suffering'.[128] Gilbreath links this with her idea that Shakespeare recognizes that we all need and desire forgiveness. Her conclusion quotes Gregory Doran agreeing: 'that is why the play is so life-affirming, and that, I think, is its special grace'. This was reflected in her statue dressed in a rich shade of green, the colour of renewal.

In 2009 Kelly Hunter appeared as Hermione in David Farr's production with Greg Hicks as Leontes.[129] When I spoke with her on Zoom (11 March 2022) we talked about the special demands of playing pregnancy in *The Winter's Tale*: her own memories of pregnancy, her desire for a realistic representation of the pregnant body, the weight and size of the pregnancy prosthesis, and her battle with the RSC's Health and Safety requirements. Figure 8 shows Hermione wearing a dress that references the simple lines of early nineteenth-century styles. The light-weight ivory-coloured cotton dress's only ornaments are a small lace trim at the neckline, a single ruffle at the hem, and a band of red ribbon tied high under the breast. The ribbon highlights the realistic shape of her ample pregnancy, which is further outlined by the contrast between the dress's soft folds at the side and the smoothness of the fabric over the extension. It seems uncontroversial, but Hunter fought two costume campaigns in this production, one for the size and weight of the pregnancy, the other for a realistic costume for the trial. Regarding the later, Hunter spoke of her determination that Hermione's appearance at the trial scene should make it clear how

---

[128] Gilbreath, 2003, 83.

[129] For trailer and photograph gallery see www.rsc.org.uk>past-productions>david-farr. This was the role that convinced Hicks that Leontes' insecurity and jealousy are 'the same kind of stuff that Shakespeare may have been sick with' interview in *Lectures de The winter's tale de William Shakespeare*, 206.

Figure 8 Realistic Pregnancy 2009 Kelly Hunter (Hermione with Mamillius), director David Farr, designer Jon Bausor. Photo: Reg Wilson ©RSC

much she has suffered from imprisonment, physically as well as mentally. Hermione had given birth under harsh conditions in prison, denied access to that baby and her son Mamillius. Hunter's traumatized Hermione was an exhausted wraith: gaunt, dirty, her hair hacked off, a bloodied bed sheet wrapped around her and wearing a soiled nightgown. The appearance was a startling transformation and the audience's gasp can be heard in the archival DVD. Her point was made, the battle won. The battle for the pregnancy costume is a different tale.

Hunter's commitment to performing Hermione with realistic physicality had different results for her in the pregnancy scenes: 1.2 and 2.1. There her determination for a realistic pregnancy prosthesis led to a battle with the RSC's Health and Safety regulations. She knew what pregnancy felt like, mentally and physically, and remembered her own pregnancy as 'a state of paradise'. Hunter had decided that Hermione was eight and a half months pregnant and wanted this stage pregnancy to feel as real as possible, including the baby's weight in utero. The plan was to use a prosthesis to recreate the weight of the baby she had carried in real life. The RSC costume workshop agreed to the experiment and made the prosthesis, and she experimented with it in rehearsal with no difficulty. The following is a summary of Kelly Hunter's description of what happened next.

At the dress rehearsal, when Hunter made her first entrance in full pregnancy regalia, she heard a voice shouting 'no, no, stop' from the back of the theatre. She had no idea who was shouting or that they were shouting at her, but saw someone running down the aisle and climbing on to the stage. It was the RSC's health and safety insurance representative, a short, slight woman who was about to do a rugby tackle to stop Hermione from moving a step further. Hunter, fully in character and much attached to this memory-induced prosthesis, tried to protect it from the woman, who was now about to reach up under her dress in order to remove the prosthesis. Hunter laughed as she remembered fighting to hold on to it, insisting: 'no this is my baby; this is Perdita'.

Health and Safety's concern was that the bulky costume might cause an accident or injure Hunter in some way or other. The very persuasive Hunter had almost convinced the inspector everything was all right, that this was the normal shape for a pregnancy. She also pointed out that the RSC could not be held responsible as she had signed a waiver taking full responsibility. But then someone noticed the prosthesis' realistic weight. The issue became the weight she was carrying. Eventually, the RSC called in Laurence Kirk, an osteopath with a speciality in repairing actors' damaged bodies and an understanding of actors' commitment to characterization. He convinced Hunter that strapping on an eight-pound weight night after night could strain her back. He pointed out that the weight may have been realistic, but a pregnant woman builds up the strength to carry it over nine months. The compromise was pink foam rubber, suitably shaped. In the archival DVD Hunter's movements are effective in conveying a heavy pregnancy. In conclusion, Hunter said she learned: 'it's not the costume. You can't rely on the costume. Shakespeare's words have to be embodied'. In this *Winter's Tale* their embodiment includes the weight of pregnancy's big belly.

The Unborn Child as New Character

.... the child brags in her belly

Loves' Labours Lost 5.2.74/5

The visibly gravid body encourages the audience to consider this presence as an entity that needs to be kept safe. Watching a heavily pregnant Hermione makes her vulnerability clearer and reinstates the part of her pregnant body that had been missing in performances between 1919 and 1969. As a stage property, the belly's extension can be embraced, stroked, protected, and be a place for Hermione to rest her arms. It also changes the way her body moves, sits, and stands. Just as an actor playing Falstaff needs to adjust to the fat suit, a Hermione needs to adjust to a pregnancy prosthesis. The size of the prosthesis is always the director's and actor's decision, and not that of the designer. Differently sized prostheses offer varying possibilities: Claire Skinner's modern-dressed Hermione at the National Theatre in 2001 was comfortable in high-end casual clothing and carried her visible belly lightly. In Cheek by Jowl's modern dress production in 2017 Natalie Radmall-Quirke's movements were restricted by her form-fitting jersey dress and enormous pregnancy. At the RSC Alexandra Gilbreath in 1999 could hardly move under the combined weight of the pregnancy and Romanov-era dress. Also at the RSC, Kelly Hunter in 2009 worked with a belly size she remembered from her own pregnancy, as did Gemma Jones in 1981, and Samantha Bond played the role during several months of her actual pregnancy in 1992. Actors talk about communicating during the performance with the prosthetic bump as though it were a living child. Imagined movements by the baby, such as a shift, a slight kick, or a false birth contraction, make Hermione pause to catch her breath, steady herself, gasp audibly, to reach out for a hand, and sometimes that hand belongs to Polixenes.

The presence of the prosthetic pregnant belly in 1969 introduced new ways for actors to develop Hermione's relationships with Leontes, Polixenes, and Mamillius. Some of the most significant and innovative uses of the prosthesis are found in productions during the decades immediately following Nunn's production. For example, Alexandra Gilbreath's Hermione in Gregory Doran's 1999 production was deeply invested in the restrictions and discomfort of her vast pregnant belly. It made her waddle when she walked, threw her off balance when she danced with Polixenes, caused her to sit with thighs spread apart, and to rest against the settee to relieve her back. She put Leontes' hand lovingly on the belly but his *tremor cordis* began when she waltzed with Polixenes, even though she kept a discreet arms-length between them. The dancing stopped when she had a series of small contractions that made her lean on him for support. These coincided with Leontes expressing jealousy, heard by the audience but not by Hermione. When the pains caused her to give a small moan, Leontes, down stage, misheard it as sexual. In David Farr's 2009 production, Kelly Hunter's Hermione and Darrell D'Silva's Polixenes have a relaxed, casual intimacy. There is just enough physical contact to be innocent but still affect a jealous mind. She easily takes his hand when talking to him. She puts her hand on his brow during their courtly dance, where they are close but with very little actual contact. She is pleased when he puts his ear to her belly, and so comfortable with him that she bumps him playfully with her belly when teasing him: 'Verily / You shall not go' (1.2.50).

Who is allowed to touch this pregnant queen's belly? Social guidelines for physical contact establish who is permitted to touch a person's body (and where), but different physical conditions can intensify the meaning of a gesture, as pregnancy does in performances of *The Winter's Tale*. Putting a hand on the gestating belly is an intimate gesture that can signify a close relationship. When Hermione places Leontes' hand there, as Gilbreath did, it is a sign of affection that acknowledges their shared bond with the unborn child. When Kelly Hunter's Hermione hugs Mamillius and places his hand there it is to connect him with the baby. The same gesture becomes more complicated when it is Polixenes' hand. It is one thing if his relationship is attentive, handing Hermione her shawl, or taking her hand, but another thing if Hermione offers this level of hand-on-the-body intimacy, even if it is only meant as a gesture of fond friendship. Details and actions such as this in one way or another have been present in nearly every performance of *The Winter's Tale* since 1969. Some productions have used interactions with the heavily pregnant body as triggers for Leontes' jealousy. For example, in 1981 at the RSC when Patrick Stewart's Leontes placed his head on Hermione's lap, the belly's size left little room for him, Ray Jewers' Polixenes then placed his own head on the other side of the lap, as though he shared equal access. At Stratford, Ontario in 1986 (set in a regal European court sometime in the 1830s) Goldie Semple's Hermione felt her baby kick, and Stephen Russell's Polixenes 'instinctively, solicitously, moved [his hand] to the place. It was bound to inflame Leontes to see evidence of "affection" in the sense of sexual instinct'.[130] At the RSC in 1986, Penny Downie 'offered an exceptionally flirtatious and ingratiating Hermione, on whom Paul Greenwood's Polixenes lavished cuddles, back-rubs, and love-lorn gazes'.[131] Gilbreath's Hermione shared a comfortably physical friendship with Ken Bones' Polixenes who acknowledged her condition's need for innocent attentions (a hand held, a peck on the cheek) while Antony Sher's Leontes ignored them and buried himself in paperwork. When Hermione left her shawl on the settee, the men's contrasting handling of it mimicked the way they treated her: Leontes crumpled it and sniffed for evidence of adultery, then threw it down. Later in the scene Polixenes picked it up, smoothed and folded it, then carried it over his arm while talking with Camillo, before putting it back. These are some of the elements in the background of Leontes' jealousy, but rarely the actual cause, which remains inexplicable.

Males Behaving Badly: Leontes and Mamillius

The Winter's Tale is a play about domestic violence, the male abuse of their power – in this case magnified by his royal position – and the effect on those who get caught up in that violence.

Gregory Doran[132]

---

[130] Warren, 1988, describing David William's production.
[131] Shrimpton, 1987, *Shakespeare Survey 40*, 177–78. [132] Doran, 2023, 49.

LEONTES:
From east, west, north and south; be it concluded,
No barricado for a belly. Know't,
It will let in and out the enemy
With bag and baggage.

The Winter's Tale 1.2.202

Leontes is always dangerous to Hermione and the unborn child. He becomes an even greater physical threat if she is big-bellied: she cannot move quickly, cannot rise easily when pushed to the floor, cannot defend herself against slaps if she needs her hands to protect the baby. His attacks on his wife are also life-threatening to the unborn child. The Leontes of Patrick Stewart (1981), John Nettles (1992), and Antony Sher (1999) in RSC productions and Cheek by Jowl's Orlando James (2016–2017) have been among the most menacing. For each of them Leontes, who is convinced this is not his baby, is enraged by the sight of his wife's pregnant body; he tells his courtiers to 'let her sport herself / With that she's big with' and tells Hermione ''tis Polixenes / Has made thee swell thus' (2.1.60-2). The following section draws on these four actors, and Christopher Wheeldon's ballet (2016), to demonstrate some of the ways that Leontes and Mamillius react aggressively to the unborn child.

Patrick Stewart

Leontes' physical abuse of Hermione has been increasingly highlighted in productions, especially when the director makes connections with current discussions of domestic violence, and, in the following examples, it is always closely linked to a significantly visible pregnancy. Actors come to Leontes' violence by different routes. Antony Sher's research in psychology, for example, showed him the dangerous insanity of the *tremor cordis*; Patrick Stewart, however, had seen it in his own father's behaviour. Even standing by his father's body in a coffin, Stewart felt as if the man 'might, at any moment, sit up and hit me'.[133] His Leontes viewed in the performance recording is full of small, scattered acts of violence directed at Hermione.

---

[133] Stewart, 2023, 294–98.

This is a very dangerous Leontes with clenched fists held rigidly at his side trying not to strike, controlling an almost overwhelming fury that is directed, in part, at the extended belly. John Barber in the *Daily Telegraph* thought it was a brilliant account of the role, including 'a real fit [that] leaves him tearful and gasping for breath, taking refuge behind a sardonic hideous grin and wild accusations' (2 July 1981). What Barber does not mention is the attacks on Hermione's body. The production opens with the exuberant finale of a court masque with Polixenes and Hermione as its king and queen, exiting off stage, followed by a cast of pastoral shepherds, shepherdesses, peasants, a dancing bear, courtiers, and musicians. An overexcited Leontes acts as the conductor, leading, directing, and, finally, applauding as Mamillius bursts triumphantly through an upstage screen, but even here Leontes seems to be on the outside directing actions that have little to do with him. The masque's high spirits, childish games, and courtly tradition create a mood that quickly changes for Leontes who begins a series of small attacks.

The first blow comes after the masque ends, while they are still in their masque costumes seen in Figure 6. Hermione is sitting with Mamillius on her left and Polixenes on her right. When Leontes enters and sees no room for him, he stands behind Hermione and pokes her repeatedly in the back. These jabs are mean, aggressive, hurt enough to make her yelp. A second attack comes soon after, when Leontes kneels beside the seated Hermione and the baby's bulk keeps him from placing his head next to her breast. It angers him that even in the womb this 'bastard' seems to push him away. When he does manage to place his head on her lap, she wraps her arm maternally around him. Polixenes then kneels on her other side, puts his head on the already crowded lap, and Hermione also puts her arm around him. Leontes' irritation mounts when Hermione teases Polixenes: 'you slipped not / With any but with us' (1.2.85). When Leontes asks, 'Is he won yet?' (1.2.85-6), he begins another series of pokes and little jabs, starting at his wife's back, but now increasing the menace by moving around her. When he pokes at the belly with two hands, Mamillius draw his toy sword ready to defend his mother. The blow comes when Leontes strikes Hermione as he remembers the 'three crabbed months' it took her to 'clap thyself my love' and utter 'I am yours for ever'. On 'yours forever'

(1.2.102-4), he pulls her hand out arms-length, then slaps it hard. When four lines later Hermione says that acceptance earned her 'a royal husband' and 'for some while a friend' Polixenes' reaction is the opposite of Leontes'. He kisses her cheek, embraces her briefly, and leads her away. Not all of Leontes' threats are physical attacks; he is dangerous even when disdainfully holding up the long sleeve of her robe.

In 2.1 Leontes' invasion into the nursery matches his vicious verbal attack with physical abuse that neither the courtiers who accompanied him nor Hermione's women are able to stop. When Hermione, puzzled by his behaviour, asks, 'What is this? Sport?' Stewart's response, directed to the attendants is that she should 'sport herself / With that she's big with' and then, to Hermione, 'Polixenes / Has made thee swell thus' (2.1.58; 60-2). With that Leontes shoves her with force from behind. When he announces to the room, 'She's an adulteress' (2.1.76), he pushes his knee into her side, dangerously near the baby. With that final assault, he races off and then storms back stopping short of actually hitting her. Hermione exits to prison accompanied by her ladies, and, unlike later productions, with no indication of the beginning of a premature birth.

John Nettles

The 1992 RSC production, directed by Adrian Noble, with John Nettles (Leontes), Samantha Bond (Hermione), and Paul Jesson (Polixenes), can be viewed in a rather blurred performance recording filmed from the back of theatre. In the promptbook the stage manager's pencilled notes for 1.2 and 2.1 clearly map a series of escalating physical attacks where the pregnancy prosthesis (the unborn child) is Leontes' target. On the promptbook's page 74 there is a note indicating that on the words 'that she's big of' (1.2.61) Leontes 'stands behind her with his arms round her on her "bump"'. The threat is that he will pull the arms too hard and tight, harming the baby. On page 75 beside 'O thou thing' the note indicates: 'Leontes hits Hermione & she falls down (or kneels) / Mamilius runs forward & shouts "No" but is pulled back by Lady (SJ) and they exit stage right followed by Lord (GW) / 3 ladies cross & kneel round'. Page 76 makes it clear how menacing Leontes is, especially each time that he stands behind Hermione. Between the play's lines 99 and 125 the stage manager notes that 'Leontes crosses and kneels behind Hermione – kisses the back of her neck – stands and turns to face her – she stands and has a birth contraction (braxton hicks). Hermione turns to go but stops and turns back to face Leontes as the lords move out of the way and the women exit'.[134]

Some of Leontes' jealousy in this production, as well as in those of other directors, is also reflected in Mamillius' reactions to the change in his mother's body. Her once comfortably sized lap has no room for him now. His is a child's uncertainty as to what the new baby will mean, fuelled by the first lady-in-waiting's teasing: 'The queen, your mother, rounds apace. We shall / Present our services to a fine new prince / One of these days, and then you'd wanton with us / If we would have you' (2.1.15-18). The sibling rivalry is acted out in different ways in productions, but the pattern is fairly standard, and the size and visibility of the prosthesis are factors. Mamillius has a child's privilege to embrace his mother, and in many productions his overactive behaviour, seems an anxious attempt to hold her attention. When he throws himself in his mother's lap here, she pulls back and pushes him away to protect the baby. He is rejected, even if temporarily, when Hermione asks her ladies to 'Take the boy to you. He so troubles me, / 'Tis past enduring' (2.1.01). The visible pregnancy becomes as threatening to him as it does to his father, and he sometimes enacts a child-size version of the parent's violence. In the promptbook, pages 71-72, Mamillius is described as running to Hermione from stage right and circling around her as she enters centre stage. He then turns back, gets a cushion out of the basket of baby things, crosses back and hits Hermione a couple of times. When she takes the pillow from him, he runs into the sheet the ladies are folding, pretending to be a ghost. While one of the ladies is untangling Mamillius from the sheet, another is caring for the seated Hermione, first removing her shoes, then massaging her neck and shoulders. Afterwards, Hermione sits on the floor so Mamillius can whisper his ghost tale in her ear. When Leontes and his men enter, she rises with effort while Leontes pulls Mamillius away from her. The stage manager's notes describing the pattern of his attack on her are quoted earlier.

---

[134] A braxton hicks is a false birth contraction.

Antony Sher

In Gregory Doran's 1999 production with Alexandra Gilbreath, the first blow to Hermione's body comes not, as might be expected from Antony Sher's Leontes, but quite unexpectedly at the beginning of 2.1 from Mamillius (Emily Bruni who also played Perdita) and are seen clearly in the DVD.[135] He is a sickly young prince, dressed in a copy of his father's uniform, confined to a wheelchair, and adores his father's masculine attention, especially their mock fights.[136] Stuck in his wheelchair, the sickly boy is uncomfortable with his mother's showers of kisses, an attention he is too old for. His age is vague but somewhere between twelve and fourteen. Earlier, 1.2, when Leontes stopped Hermione embracing the boy (the size of her belly and fullness of her dress were suffocating). Mamillius' reaction was relief touched with disdain. Later he listens to Leontes' accusations against his mother, but the boy does not show his response to them until the beginning of 2.1. Then, as Mamillius is wheeled in by an attendant and has his mother walking beside him, he deliberately strikes her breast. When he turns away (towards the audience and the camera), the satisfied look on his face shows it was deliberate. The blow startles Hermione who draws away, keeping her hand on the breast. He has bruised her emotionally and physically. She makes no reference to it, but it explains why she asks her ladies to take him away because 'He bothers me'. Settled, she calls him back to her and prepares to hear his story. 'There was a man ... ' is the cue for Leontes to storm into this already tense nursery.

Antony Sher was best known for what Paul Taylor called his dependable ability to 'absolutely dominate the stage', and the critic was surprised by Sher's 'rich and complex characterization' of Leontes (*Independent*, 7 January 1999). Sher felt that 'the rage and destructiveness in Leontes' [isn't about] "evil" behaviour; this is about someone in trouble, in pain'.[137] The restraint on physical violence in 1.2 was part of his control of the role in 'an interpretation crammed with interpretive points'. In 1.2 the anger is directed

---

[135] Commercial DVD performance recording. [136] See Rutter, 2007, 108–11.

[137] Sher, 2003, 'Leontes in *The Winter's Tale* and *Macbeth*' in *Players of Shakespeare 5*. 94.

at objects: he scratches a record by dragging the needle across it while Hermione and Polixenes dance; when Hermione leaves her shawl on the settee to walk with Polixenes, Leontes crumples it up after sniffing it for clues of adultery. His Leontes is 'muted, tense and anxious, troubled rather than overwhelmed' until he bursts into the nursery and turns his fury into an attack on Hermione's body and the pregnancy. When he enters, just as Mamillius starts his story, his appearance shocks Hermione. She rises, but her attempts to embrace him are rejected. Instead, with his fist raised ready to strike, he pushes her across the stage with a series of shoves until she falls to the floor. She gets up slowly, keeping one hand on her belly and the other on her back. When she approaches her husband, he throws her back down. No one dares move to her rescue. When she holds out her hand in reconciliation, also asking for his help to stand, he refuses, stares, turns, and leaves. This has the impact of another blow, while the earlier one has started a painful miscarriage. She needs her ladies' support as she exits, debilitated by the premature contractions.

Orlando James

Cheek by Jowl's 2016 production, directed by Declan Donnellan, which foregrounded domestic violence, also used a blow resulting in a miscarriage. Orlando James' Leontes is pathologically vicious, quick to anger, and brutal in attack, aligned with Tom Cawte's equally pathologically distraught Mamillius, a boy weeping in anger, flailing in terror.[138] Natalie Radmall-Quirke's Hermione seems able to keep him in balance, at least before the *tremor cordis* strikes him. She handles his quirks skilfully, with affection and intelligence, but always keeping a watchful and apprehensive eye on both him and Mamillius.

She also carries a full-term pregnancy, accentuated by a body-hugging jersey dress seen in Figure 9, where the furious Leontes twists Hermione's arm behind her back, forcing her body backwards; at that angle the pregnant belly fills the centre of the image. In the production there is no indication of where or when the action is taking place. The stage is bare

---

[138] The livestream capture, 19 April 2017, Barbican Theatre London, can be accessed through Cheek by Jowl's website's education page and YouTube.

Performing Visible Pregnancy in Shakespeare's Plays 73

Figure 9 Leontes' Rage 2017 Orlando James (Leontes) Natalie Radmall-Quirke (Hermione) Tom Cawte (Mamillius), director Declan Donnellen, designer Nick Ormerod. Screen Grab, Cheek by Jowel's livestream 2024.

except for a white-painted wooden crate, about eight feet long, that serves as a wide bench. The only backdrop is a partition made of similar narrow boards. Clothing is contemporary, but without the elegant casualness of cashmere sweaters and bespoke shoes seen in Nicholas Hytner's Sicilian court. In Donnellan's production both kings' clothes could have come from the mid-price sales rack. Their ordinariness could make it seem of no particular importance, except that the designer Nick Ormerod is a master of the subtle use of contemporary dress. The clothing's anonymity is deliberately puzzling. In the opening minutes there is a 'dumb show' where Leontes and Polixenes chase around and wrestle, and the only sound is their thudding feet. At that point, with Hermione and Mamillius looking on approvingly, it is not clear who is Sicilia and who is Bohemia. Eventually Leontes is identified as the more unbuttoned of the two, dressed in a button-down collar shirt with rolled-up sleeves and jeans, while Polixenes is more constrained in a long-sleeved white shirt buttoned at the wrist and neck, trousers and a dark tie knotted tightly at the throat. Mamillius is in standard adolescent 'proper' dress, in white shirt, tie, and trousers, but this suggests a separation from Leontes through its similarity to Polixenes' clothes. In contrast to their casually dressed king, the palace staff (not present in 1.2) are dressed appropriately in well-tailored black suits for Camillo and other courtiers and black skirts, white blouses, and heels for Hermione's ladies-in-waiting.

Central to the action and motivation in 1.2 and 2.1, Hermione's pregnancy costume (Figure 9) holds the viewer's eye. The shape of the pregnancy prosthesis is large, certainly a sufficient size to hold a healthy well-developed baby who will be a 'lusty babe, likely to live' (2.2.25). The bulky belly extends out from Radmall-Quirke's slender frame and makes it difficult for her to move. It seems to tire Hermione, who gives it nearly constant attention, stroking, wrapping arms around it, supporting it, or resting an arm or a hand there. It hampers, hinders, and distracts her. This has been true in other productions discussed here, but what makes it compelling and unique is the effect of her costume, a dress that clings so closely to the body's shape that it seems to bring the baby forward, even into a place of danger. The question is why this particular, relatively ordinary, dress becomes so important. It is a type of dress that can be purchased at a range of prices, and hers looks moderately expensive. The quality of the fabric and the shape of the draped tucks over the bust suggest it is more Harvey Nichols or Saks Fifth Avenue than the High Street or local mall. Its style is still popular, eight years later, so there is nothing extraordinary about it then or now. The colour is a subtle brown/grey, the sleeves long, the jewellery a simple double strand of pearl-size beads at the modest neckline and small earrings. Her stockings are sheer and dark, her shoes mid-heeled and her hair in a simple, but well-styled, French twist. It is an appropriately polished look, but the body-clinging dress also reflects an extraordinary time for fashion in maternity dressing: the public presentation of the pregnant belly in a socially acceptable garment whose thinness accentuates the naked outline of its every curve. This plain dress sheaths Hermione's body as if it were the body's own skin. Its modern visual roots go back to the 1991 *Vanity Fair* cover by Annie Liebowitz featuring a naked Demi Moore, nine months pregnant, seated in profile. Publishing the photograph on the cover of a major magazine was a signifier of a cultural shift towards liberated pregnancy, although many found the cover shocking, and some newsstands refused to display it.[139] Except, the shape of this Hermione's body nearly bursting with pregnancy also evokes the primal images of ancient fertility carvings.

In the production, this primal image of pregnancy fits well with the intensity of Leontes' and Mamillius' anxiety-ridden fury. The space claimed by Hermione's body, and her attention paid to it, displaced them. She has become an embodiment of the ancient female figure, fruitful in both body and mind, who would have been too powerful and, therefore, 'threatening to the supremacy of male imagination'.[140] Most critics, including Dominic Cavendish, thought Leontes was 'suffering, plainly, from man-child feelings of displacement (*Daily Telegraph*, 7 April 2017). Adult actor Tom Cawte's disturbed Mamillius (convincingly aged between twelve and fourteen) had even deeper behavioural disorders that resulted in his screaming tantrums and terrified rages. Stephen Purcell noted that the boy 'seemed distressed by the thought of his mother's pregnancy and [. . . .] that the king suffered from a similar disorder to his son'.[141] Lynn Gardiner observed that 'For both man and boy, love of Hermione goes hand-in-hand with possession of Hermione' (*Guardian*, 4 October 2017). The queen is plagued by her son's emotional imbalance, as well as the quiet thrumming undercurrent of Leontes' volatility. In the nursery the boy throws himself on the floor in tantrums and the two ladies-in-waiting try to quiet him. The sobs and screams stop only when one of them randomly plays on a toy piano, but begin again when she teases him about the new prince who will take his place. The boy is completely terrified and only calms down when Hermione brings him to sit beside her on the bench. He settles into her arms, stretches out on the bench, but before he starts to whisper his story to her, he kicks out hard at her ladies sitting beside him, forcing them to leave the bench: 'Yon grasshoppers shall not hear it' (2.1.31). Hermione gives them an apologetic look asking for understanding and conveying 'you know how he is' as Leontes enters.

Nearly every critic cites the ultimate moment of Leontes' attack on Hermione in the nursery when he hits her so hard it causes a miscarriage. It

---

[139] Hearn, 2020, 118–19. [140] Filippini, 2021, 1–39. [141] Purcell, 2018, 307.

is reported variously that he 'kicks her' (*Time Out*), 'knee[s] her' (*Daily Telegraph*), 'takes a running kick at the stomach' (*Independent*), and 'smashes his fist into her pregnant belly (*The Times*). On the recorded performance, the knee slams into the belly. This is the climax of a stream of escalated attacks, from a man whose affectionate embraces and kisses could feel like a blow. Leontes was extremely physical, always in motion, quick to push or punch. When Mamillius pestered him once too often, his response was to punch the boy hard enough to knock him down. When the courtier Camillo would not agree to poison Polixenes, he was thrown to the ground, straddled by Leontes and saved himself from the threatened punch to the face by agreeing. Whereupon Leontes helped him to his feet, embraced him, and kissed him on the mouth. His lightest blow to Hermione was to flick her nose with his finger, his most visually dramatic was to pull her hair so hard her body arched backwards. His eeriest violation of boundaries occurred in 1.2 when, struck by the *tremor cordis* he described his wife's infidelities as he moved Polixenes and Hermione around like showroom dummies. Polixenes and Hermione sat a few feet apart on the bench and, as the lighting changes to blue, they froze. Leontes accenuated his claims by rearranging the position of their limbs and expressions on their faces. On 'paddling palms and pinching fingers' he stretched out their arms so their hands touched and wiggled their fingers; on 'making practiced smiles' he turned their heads toward each other and pulled the mouths awry'; on 'then to sigh' he squeezed their chests until they wheezed' (1.2.115, 116, 117). Eventually he moved their bodies into a coital position, where he moved them back and forth, Hermione's mouth opening at each thrust engineered by Leontes the puppet master. The culminating moment of these displays of irrational violence came, not with the blow that caused the miscarriage, but with Hermione's response to it. Sitting on the floor, dazed, in shock and gasping for breath she reached up under her dress to check; when she withdrew the hand it was covered with blood. In a moment as pagan as any in mythology, she turned to Mamillius who was sitting next to her; soundlessly and expressionlessly she smeared her blood across his face and eyes. For a moment it had become a Greek tragedy. Nothing that followed was as powerful.

The Royal Ballet, Christopher Wheeldon Choreographer

Christopher Wheeldon's *The Winter's Tale*, an extraordinarily successful version of the play, parallels Declan Donnellan's production in interesting ways, particularly the centrality of the pregnant belly/unborn baby as an object of violence. Stephen Purcell's description of Cheek by Jowl's *Winter's Tale* in *Shakespeare Survey* as a 'pared down, starkly symbolic staging, combining full-bodied emotional realism with stylized ensemble choreography' could equally be describing Wheeldon's version.[142] The ballet, a coproduction of London's Royal Ballet and The National Ballet of Canada, premiered at the Royal Opera House in 2014, was revived there in 2016 and 2024, and is now regarded as one of the classic Shakespeare ballets, alongside *A Midsummer Night's Dream* and *Romeo and Juliet*. The following reference material is linked to the 2016 production and is drawn from interviews with Wheeldon and Joby Talbot, the ballet's composer, performance reviews (Hermione danced by Lauren Cuthbertson, Leontes by Edward Watson), and the commercial DVD of that production.[143] It was Nicholas Hytner (director of the play at the National Theatre in 2001) who suggested *Winter's Tale* to Wheeldon sometime around 2011 when they discussed the choreographer's desire to create a new Shakespeare ballet. For this play, the ballet would need to create new scenes for events described but not seen on stage, including the death of Mamillius. It would also have to slim down the play, cut some scenes, shorten others, create new ones, remove some characters, minimize others, keep the corps de ballet in mind as well as lead dancers.[144] In Wheeldon's two-hour ballet, the core of the plot remains understandable, beautifully organized and dramatically conveyed, though he thought a viewer would still benefit from reading the programme notes before watching. The ballet also places a heavily

---

[142] Purcell, 2018, 307.

[143] *The Royal Ballet: The Winter's Tale*, 2015, Opus Arte, DVD Extras.

[144] For interview with Wheeldon, see Lyndsey Winship, www.theguardian/stage/2016/mar/07/the-winters-tale-christopher-wheeldon-shakespeare. For interview with Talbot, see www.gramaphone.co.uk/feature/jody-talbot-talks-about-his-groundbreaking-ballet-score-for-the-winters-tale. January 20, 2015.

pregnant Hermione at the centre of relationships and actions. Joan Acocella, writing in the *New Yorker*, was very aware of this focus and describes how in the opening scenes Leontes, Polixenes and Hermione 'repeatedly dance enlaced, with the belly as a sort of fourth participant, the product, it might seem, of all their loves'.[145] Leontes suffers the *tremor cordis* attack during this 'enlaced' dance when Hermione places his hand on one side of her pregnant belly and then puts Polixenes' on the other side. Wheeldon explains: 'She feels the baby's kicking and she wants to share it with them'.[146] Hermione is radiantly happy, but Leontes stares at his hand as if something is wrong with what it is feeling and jerks it back as if he is touching something infected. The child moving in Hermione's womb feels wrong to him; it cannot be his. The idea takes over, twists his body, makes his fingers into spiders, his limbs out of control, and leaves him shattered. This becomes a 'ballet bruto'. First he attacks Polixenes, throws him on the ground, stamps on him, tries to throttle him, and, when courtiers pull him off, he exits and returns with a knife. He then acts out the jealousy in a series of violent attacks aimed at the unborn child, even before the nursery scene where the worst violence usually occurs in productions. The pregnant belly is large, and appropriately of a size close to giving birth. Even descriptions of just a few of the dance moments convey the overwhelming abuse. His movements are sharp, angular, flexed-feet jumps, kicks that stab, elbows held at sharp angles. Even the skirt of his knee-length jacket lashes out dangerously as he twirls. Leontes keeps trying to wrap his arms around the belly in order to apply enough pressure to kill it. Acocella describes Hermione's arabesques seeming 'pinioned to a rack of pain'. At one point there is a series of short steps where Hermione, using all her strength, manages to hold his arms open and away from it, but at other times the arms are around it, and also under it, even lifting her entire torso up above his shoulders. Shakespeare wrote vicious speeches for Leontes' attacks on Hermione, but seeing them translated into stylized dance movements makes the brutality vivid and relentless. It starts

[145] Acocella, 2016, 79.
[146] 'Extras', *The Royal Ballet: The Winter's Tale*, 2015, Opus Arte, DVD.

before he enters the nursery and explodes further there, and it lasts long because the movements must convey his earliest suspicions as well as later convictions.

Acocella emphasizes the role the pregnant belly plays in the ballet: 'Hermione's condition is very much stressed. Once she is accused of adultery, she keeps running her hand over her belly, as if to say to Leontes, "How can you doubt me? Look at the fruit of our love". He stares at that belly thinking it contains 'Polixenes' child and this not only enrages him further; troublingly, it also seems to excite him a little. [...] Later he almost rapes the very pregnant Hermione. Even as he denounces Hermione, he buries his face in her abdomen'.[147] Elizabeth Klett describes Leontes' public accusations of infidelity as a 'series of grand jetés and powerful developpé kicks diagonally across the stage towards Hermione, pointing an accusing finger continually'. Klett later lists the steps in a combative pas de deux where Leontes grabs Hermione's hands and pulls them out in front of her so that 'she counter balances against him, circling her leg in a series of *ronds de jambe*. [...] He jerks her forward, pulls on her hands, forces her to hop awkwardly by pushing from behind, then 'clutches the sides of her torso with his elbows [...]. His hands are claws on either side of the pregnant belly'.[148] He throws her to the floor (the near rape Acocella refers to), gets on top of her, and when she tries to crawl out from under, pulls her back by the leg. Mamillius runs in and tries to pull her to safety. At his signal, Leontes' officers toss the queen back and forth between them, until shielding her stomach, she falls. She refuses to allow them to touch her, and insists on the dignity of walking to prison without being forced, but, finally, nearly collapsing, she needs help from Paulina.

In the play the boy's death takes place off stage and is announced by a Servant who interrupts the trial: 'O sir, I shall be hated to report it / The prince your son, with mere conceit and fear / Of the queen's speed, is gone'. Shakespeare gives Leontes' a two-word response: 'How, "gone"?' which is matched by the Servant's two words: 'Is dead' (3.2.140-45). Wheeldon

---

[147] Acocella, 2016, 78–79. [148] See Klett, 2020, 13, 138.

covers this by giving Leontes a dance of mourning holding his son's body. Mamillius dies on stage watching the trial, having crept downstairs carrying his teddy bear and hiding in the shadows. This is among the many invented scenes Wheeldon inserted to present material described but not shown. Bob Crowley's costume worked together with the dancing in the opening scene to convey Shakespeare's information about the kings' boyhood friendship, their falling in love, their young princes, the arrival in Sicilia of Polixenes, his decision to leave, its reversal at Hermione's persuasion. Crowley's costumes for Hermione, all in deep purple, are all variations on a dress with a single line that starts with a leotard-style top and flows into a longish skirt. Hermione appears in a succession of costumes aligned to her own history: the dress is calf-length and she is flat-bellied when she is younger and being wooed, shown as the mother of Mamillius, and as the queen welcoming Polixenes at the start of his visit. Indicating a mid-point in this visit, the original dress is overlaid by another with a gathered panel at the front that draws attention to a small but visible pregnancy bump. Finally, at the point where the original play begins, she is heavily pregnant in an ankle length version of the dress, but now, without the gathered panel of cloth. The ample size of the belly needs nothing further to draw attention to it. It is clear that the sight of Hermione's body enrages but also excites him.

After the intensity of the earlier, Sicilian, section of the ballet, the final scene seems almost anti-climactic, until its final moment. The statue of Hermione is next to an effigy of Mamillius which remains there when she comes alive and steps down from the platform. Her pas de deux of reconciliation with Leontes is at first tentative then sinuous. Paulina dances around the reunited families, performing a series of slow arabesques and reaching her hands up imploringly, perhaps invoking the dead child. As Hermione and Perdita leave, Leontes turns back to Mamillius' statue, reaches towards it longingly. Paulina shakes her head, gestures for him to follow the others. She stays, and stretches out prone before the statue, then bends her torso forward, sweeping her arms over her head as the curtain falls. The final image is the boy's statue, a black silhouette against a swirling red background (139–140). Declan Donnellan also ended Cheek by Jowl's production with Mamillius. Before he exited the boy walked, unseen, around the reunited living, unable to reach out to them. An important point of Shakespeare's play is Hermione's absolute forgiveness, the joy (or peace) of reconciliation and perhaps even salvation. In productions such as these, where Leontes' attacks become so deeply, physically vicious, it is much harder to accept Shakespeare's ending. Wheeldon and Donnellan's conclusions, focused on the presence of the dead boy, leave a trace of the unforgiveable; they are a reminder of the collateral damage of Leontes' actions that were made even more sadistic by Hermione's visible pregnancy. The memory of what has been seen cannot be reversed and skews the ending.

6 The Pregnant Actress: *The Comedy of Errors* 2021. A Conversation with Phillip Breen and Hedydd Dylan

What happens to a Shakespeare production if the lead actor's pregnancy will become visible at some point during the run? The director's usual step is to replace her; the rare exceptions when the actor stays are informative, but seldom explored. For example, in the 1992 RSC production directed by Adrian Noble, the pregnant Samantha Bond was able to play Hermione in *The Winter's Tale* almost up to giving birth because her costume for the first two acts was designed to show the pregnant character's gravid body. In the 1998 New York Shakespeare Festival's *Cymbeline* (a 12-day limited run, August 4–16) directed by Andrei Serban. Imogen was played by Stephanie Roth Haberle who was seven-and-a-half months pregnant. Serban was pleased with the situation: 'Stephanie carries life inside her. It is very touching'. It's not a metaphor; it's real. From night to night, you don't know. She could give birth.[149] Her first costume was a loose white smock, and her second costume was men's clothing layered to minimize her shape. The pregnancy was undisguised, but also ignored as there was little reason to integrate it.

A far more intensive and complicated process took place when the actor Hedydd Dylan's actual pregnancy was made a central element of the

---

[149] *New York Times*, 'Theater: a New 'Cymbeline' of Moon, Grass and Trees', by Andrea Stevens, August 16, 1998.

character she played in Phillip Breen's 2021 RSC production of *The Comedy of Errors*. Phillip Breen and Hedydd Dylan discussed the production with me a few months after the London run ended.[150] Enfolding Dylan's actual pregnancy into a non-pregnant role was an innovative approach that excited both of them and made it possible for her to perform throughout the pregnancy; she stayed in the production almost until it closed. The play is Shakespeare's comedy of two sets of identical twin brothers (each set a servant and his employer), separated in infancy, eventually reunited after a series of mistaken identities.

A pregnant Adrianna was not part of the director's original plans when rehearsals began eight weeks before the covid-related suspension of all London theatre work. When rehearsals finally resumed, Hedydd Dylan was pregnant and thought she would have to leave the show. Breen, not wanting to lose Dylan's performance, was intrigued with the idea that the pregnancy 'fitted brilliantly' with the various elements of doubleness he was including in the production. The director shaped the interpretation of the role around Dylan's pregnancy. Adrianna would be a woman close to giving birth (which Dylan would be by the end of the run), and it could provide a reason for her anxiety about her neglectful husband, her fear of losing her attractiveness, and her angry, tearful outbursts. Peter Kirwan wrote in his review that having 'Adrianna visibly pregnant was transformative to the play, making [her husband] Antipholus of Ephesus' philandering seem even more cruel'.[151] Breen thought the pregnancy could also help to identify her husband's behaviour as part of his own anxieties about fatherhood. It was a 'fluke' but the groundwork was already there in the planned doubling in the set design, the accompanying music, and some of the casting. Dylan explained that the costume included a large pregnancy prosthesis during her early months, was adjusted 'as the baby grew into the bump' and eventually discarded when her own body reached

---

[150] All comments, unless noted otherwise, are drawn from conversations with Breen and Dylan. See RSC "Such Nativity!" Adrianna's Pregnancy in the Comedy of Errors. See also www.phillipbreen.com.

[151] Kirwan, 2022, *Shakespeare Survey 75*, 350. See also Lennox, 2022, *Shakespeare Bulletin* vol 4, no. 2, 275–9.

Figure 10 Incorporating Actual Pregnancy 2021, *Comedy of Errors*, Hedydd Dylan (Adrianna), director Phillip Breen, designer Max Jones. Photo: Peter Le May ©RSC

a similar size. To her, the prosthesis felt protective and was 'an outer shell' shielding the baby.

The director, actor and costume designer worked out the details including a maternity costume that emphasized the body with a clinging jersey dress and a bolero top tied under the bust, its contrasting print further highlighting the big-bellied shape seen on Hedydd Dylan as Adrianna in Figure 10. A 1980s big-hair blonde wig added to the exaggeration of her size, enough to be comic but not cartoonish. Dylan described how she rejected the designer's original proposal of 'a

Princess Diana smock': 'I fought hard against that and told him to just dress me as if I wasn't pregnant; give me 80s power shoulders and make me glam'. This, she knew, would be 'more interesting than making pregnancy sexless', and it had already been decided in rehearsals that pregnancy 'increased Adrianna's sex drive'. It was also decided that this was a new marriage of only a year or two and still in a honeymoon stage. Expecting a baby had unsettled the couple, providing an explanation for Adrianna's insecurity and anger. On stage, Dylan felt the sympathy, and sometimes the anger, that came particularly from the women in the audience at the husband's (possibly chaste) visits to the Courtesan.

The production's long run meant that as the baby grew, its movements became part of her performances: 'I don't think it [her performance] changed when he [the baby] started to move on stage; it was as if an extra plate was spinning'. Speaking about the experience, she made it clear why this worked so well for her and the production company. She enjoyed working and continuing to 'be myself'; it felt 'powerful to play a demanding role and to be 'active and earning money'. The acting company responded warmly to the pregnancy, but at the start she did have to convince people that she was not an invalid.

Balancing the play's slap-stick violence was taken into account with satisfying results, especially since it was not physically domestic violence. Breen has made his career working with comedy and said he 'cannot bear to see the comedy characters being robbed of their complex psychology'. The pregnancy was treated lightly for humour, but without any hint of fat-shaming. Dylan found ways to incorporate what she was experiencing as a pregnant woman, including the physical limitations imposed by a large belly. Her Adrianna deals with some of them, including a yoga session led by Dr Pinch (imagined here as a guru). Yoga postures previously easy no longer worked, despite her cheerful attempts. In one of the play's funniest scenes, the size of the belly lets her physically dominate as she berates the man she thinks is her husband but is actually his twin. With an unstoppable tirade of abuse, she looms over the bewildered man who is trapped at his restaurant table by her body. At that moment, Adrianna resembled one the great-bellied women described in *Henry VIII* who pushed through the crowd using their bellies as battering rams in a battle.

The final scene, in which everyone is reunited and reconciled, includes the revelation that the local Abbess is the long-lost mother of the two Antipholus and the expected baby is her grandchild. In the Abbess' invitation for everyone to join her at a 'gossips' feast' (5.1.405) Breen stayed focused on the theme of pregnancy and birth and specifically kept the Folio's word 'nativity' instead of using its frequent replacement 'festivity'. When the Abbess placed her hand on Adrianna's belly she said, 'After so long grief, such nativity' (5.1.406).[152]

Breen believes that comedy and tragedy are a binary, and the real skill of playing comedy is 'the heart-breaking deep seriousness' of this 'secular miracle that ends the play'. No one involved with the production had expected the impact the pregnancy would have on the company. Dylan was surprised by the way the acting company became a community even more than usual because of the shared experience of the actual pregnancy. At the centre was Dylan's own pregnant body and the changes she (and it) went through were incorporated into the role. A few weeks before Dylan gave birth, Naomi Sheldon took on the role and buckled on the pregnancy prosthesis, and they job-shared. The director's celebratory last-night speech included: 'One of the miracles of this *Comedy of Errors* was the birth of young Talliesin Boyd Step', Dylan's baby born on the 14th of December.[153]

7 Epilogue

Tell me, mine own, / Where has thou been preserved / Where lived? How found.

Hermione, *The Winter's Tale* 5.3.124

Once visible pregnancy returned to *The Winter's Tale* in Trevor Nunn's production, costumes that included a pregnancy prosthesis became

---

[152] The word 'nativity' is used in the *Folio*, but has often been changed by editors and directors to 'festivity' to avoid repetition. See note 404, 406 (p. 300) in Cartwright, ed., 2016, Shakespeare, *The Comedy of Errors*.

[153] Full text available on w.w.w.phillipbreen.com.

a familiar sight in other Shakespeare's plays.[154] The device has been used in *Macbeth* to increase Lady Macduff's vulnerability, used in *As You Like It* to turn Audrey into a clichéd pregnant bride, used for Helena in *All's Well That Ends Well* where a visibly gravid body supports her announcement of pregnancy. In *Love's Labours Lost* a visible pregnancy can make it clear what is meant when Jaquenetta is said to be 'quick' with child.[155] A pregnant woman has also become a familiar figure in *Measure for Measure* as part of Mistress Overdone's bawdy entourage. The RSC staging of Maggie Farrell's *Hamnet* included a lyrical scene in which Shakespeare's young wife transitioned into her first pregnancy. Anne stood still at centre stage while two women moved forward from the far edge at either side of the stage holding the ends of a long piece of fabric; they moved slowly, as if in a dream, towards her as they folded the fabric over and over until it formed a thick rounded cushion that they tied around her waist so that Anne was pregnant in the scene that followed.[156]

Today's politics of pregnancy include issues related to legal abortion, infertility, surrogate mothers, and celebrity pregnancies. By 2015 the 'baby bump' had become a highly desirable fashion accessory.[157] It had also been monetized through the use of pregnant celebrities in advertisements selling related goods. One advertising campaign for pregnancy test kits features celebrities posing with their positive test results. Red-carpet social and award events continue to provide 'unusually uncloistered moments' for the so-called pregnancy 'bump' (Ellie Violet Bramley, *Guardian* 13 July 2024). There is a trend for star-status mothers-to-be to

---

[154] There are first-hand reports of the tie-on apron used for costume fittings with pockets marked 'three months', 'six months', 'nine months' that hung in the RSC costume shop during the 1980s. The company now outsources the prosthesis.

[155] The RSC's *Love's Labours Lost*, (11 April–18 May 2024) signalled her pregnancy with morning sickness. Emily Burns, dir.

[156] *Hamnet*, adapted by Lolita Chakrabarti; director Erica Whyman, opened April 2023.

[157] See Cramer, 2021, 'The Baby Bump is the New Birkin', in *Fashion Talks: Undressing the Power of Style*.

attend celebrity events dressed in maternity designs that feature the full belly. Outfits are draped, transparent, slit or use cutouts offering in the flesh views of the bulge.[158] There is also a new, darker twist entering the pregnancy narrative. According to Becca Rothfield, pregnancy has become 'the subject of a great deal of body horror for fairly obvious reasons [….] as gruesome in their own way as the grisliest conceit of Cronenberg's [horror] films.'[159] This includes women for whom being pregnant provokes a frightening sense of loss of control over their body. It is the foetus as alien monster with a bit of *Rosemary's Baby* (demon spawn). Running parallel to this is increasing information on medical mismanagement, often resulting in severe damage to the woman or the child. Pregnancy is presented as not only uncomfortable but dangerous, which brings the politics of pregnancy in synch with the cultural anxieties of the times. Since performance and its costumes are always touched by their times, one wonders how this changing cultural narrative will affect Hermione in her pregnancy.

Carol Chillington Rutter points out that 'actresses are political; they have helped redefine how women are portrayed on the stage, and they have shaped how our decade sees Shakespeare's roles'. They also 'want audiences to leave the theatre not with answers, but with question marks hanging over their heads'.[160] It is assumed that pregnancy will remain visible, but what else might actresses do with it? Ellen Kean and Mary Anderson's Victorian and Edwardian sentimental portrayals were replaced by Judi Dench's youthful mother, whose happy pregnancy was nuanced. In later performance a more sizable and uncomfortable prosthesis restricted movements of Alexandra Gilbreath's and Kelly Hunter's Hermione. Is Natalie Radmall-Quirke's Hermione who nervously protected her belly a transitional darker version that will influence other performances? Will there be Hermiones who are fretted by their pregnancy and snappish (as

---

[158] See Daisy Jones, 'Every Star Who's Aced Pregnancy Dressing on the Met Gala Red Carpet', *Vogue* 9 May 2025. www.vogue.co.uk.
[159] Rothfield, Becca (2024) *All Things Are Too Small*. London: Virago.
[160] Rutter, 1988, xii; xxxvii.

Shakespeare makes her when Mamillius is annoying); will they be bored with trying to placate Leontes or barely able to tolerate having to be charming to Polixenes? Perhaps these Hermiones will be fed up with men behaving like the overgrown boys seen in recent productions. If this happens, what part will their pregnancy costume play?

List of Abbreviations

NT   National Theatre
RSC   Royal Shakespeare Company
SBT   Shakespeare Birthplace Trust

References

Information on RSC productions is available online at Shakespeare Birthplace Trust Collection.

https://collections.shakespeare.org.uk/search/rsc performances/view_as/grid/search/everywhere:the-winters-tale.

Archives consulted included

SBT archives RSC *The Winter's Tale* Costume Plots & Costume Bibles:1976, 1986, 1992, 1999.

Chris Dyer costume designs, 1981. Costume Bibles not available for examination: 1981, 1984, 2010.

SBT archives RSC, *The Winter's Tale* Promptbooks: 1943, 1948, 1960, 1969, 1976, 1992, 1999.

SBT archives RSC, *The Winter's Tale* Production Photographs: 1943, 1960, Royal Shakespeare Company: 1969, 1976, 1981, 1984, 1986, 1992, 1993, 1999.

SBT archives RSC, *The Winter's Tale* Archival DVDs: 1976, 1982, 1986, 1993, 2010.

National Theatre, *The Winter's Tale*, dir. Nicholas Hytner, NT archive, performance recording 2001.

Cheek by Jowl, *The Winter's Tale*. Livestream recording, Barbican Theatre, 19 April 2017, director Declan Donnellan, designer, Nick Ormerod. Accessed through www.Cheek by Jowl.

SBT archives, RSC *Measure for Measure* performance 1984, director Steve Pimlott, recording and photographs.

Odéon, Paris, Zadek production, *Measure for Measure* 1991 archive photographs.

Cheek by Jowl, *Measure for Measure*. Livestream recording, April 2019, director Declan Donnellan, designer, Nick Ormerod. Accessed through www.cheekbyjowl.com.

SBT Archives RSC *All's Well That Ends Well*, performance recording 2013, 1993; photograph files: 2013, 1993, 1992.

Commercial Release DVD

The Winter's Tale (2007) Thanhouser Company Film Preservation, DVD volumes 7, 8, & 9. Portland, OR.

The Winter's Tale (2014) The Royal Ballet, choreography, Christopher Wheeldon, music composer, Jay Talbot, set and costume, Bob Crowley, performance recorded April 2014, Royal Opera House. London: Opus Arte.

The Winter's Tale, RSC, 1999 director. Gregory Doran, costumes Robert Jones.

Other Sources

Acocella, Joan (2016) 'A Rain of Fire: Christopher Wheeldon's "*Winter's Tale*"'. *The New Yorker*, 22 August 2016, 79.

Aebischer, Pascale (2012) *Performing Early Modern Drama Today*. Cambridge: Cambridge University Press.

Allam, Roger. (1993) '*The Duke in Measure forMeasure*' in *Players of Shakespeare*. Cambridge: Cambridge University Press. 21–41.

Altman, Joel B. (2023) *Shakespeare the Bodger: Ingenuity, Imitation and the Arts of the Winter's Tale*. Edinburgh: Edinburgh University Press.

Anderson, Mary (1896) *A Few More Memories*. London: Hutchinson. Reprint 1936.

Asleon, Robyn (1999) *Sarah Siddons and Her Portraitists*. Los Angeles: J. Paul Getty Museum.

Baker, Herschel Clay (1942) *John Philip Kemble: The Actor in His Theatre*. New York: Greenwood Press.

Ball, William Hamilton (1968) *Shakespeare on Silent Film: A Strange Eventful History*. New York: Theatre Arts Books.

Barbieri, Donatella (2017) *Costume in Performance: Materiality, Culture and the Body*. London: Bloomsbury.

Bartholomeusz, Dennis (1982) *The Winter's Tale in Performance in England and America, 1611–1976*. Cambridge: Cambridge University Press.

Behl, Dennis (1994) 'A Career in the Theatre', in T. J. Edelstein. *The Stage Is All the World: The Theatrical Designs of Tanya Moiseiwitsch*. Chicago, IL: The David and Alfred Smart Museum, University of Chicago, 30–126.

Bethell, S. L. (1947) *The Winter's Tale: A Study*. Charlottesville: University of Virginia.

Bicks, Caroline (2003) *Midwiving Subjects in Shakespeare's England*. Women and Gender in the Early Modern World. Surrey: Ashgate.

Boaden, James (1827) *Memoirs of Sarah Siddons*. 2 vols. London: Henry Colburn, reprint Cambridge University Press, 2013.

Braunmuller, A. R. (2020) 'Introduction', *Measure for Measure*. The Arden Shakespeare. London: Bloomsbury. Reprint 2024.

Buchanan, Judith (2009) *Shakespeare on Silent Film*. Cambridge: Cambridge University Press.

Burzyka, Katazyna (2022) *Pregnant Bodies from Shakespeare to Ford: A Phenomenology of Pregnancy in English Early Modern Drama*. Routledge Studies in Literature and Health Humanities. London: Routledge.

Campbell, Thomas (1834) *Life of Siddons*. 2 vols. London: Effingham Wilson.

Carlyle, Carol Jones (2000) *Helen Faucit: Fire and Ice on the Victorian Stage*. London: Society for Theatre Research.

Carpenter, John (2023) '"One of the Last of the Classical Actresses": Lillah McCarthy (1875–1960)', in *Theatre Notebook* 77.1. Trevor R. Griffiths, Gabriel Egan & Anselm Heinrich, eds. London: Society for Theatre Research, 8–25.

Castaldo, Annalisa & Knight, Rhonda, eds. (2018) *Stage Matters: Props, Bodies, and Space in Shakespearean Performance*. Madison: Farleigh Dickinson University Press.

Cole, John William (1859) *The Life and Theatrical Times of Charles Kean*, 2 vol. London: Richard Bentley.

Cowden Clark, Charles and Mary, eds. (1898) *Cassell Family Shakespeare*. London: Cassell, Petter and Galpin.

Cramer, Renee Ann (2015) *Pregnant with the Stars: Watching and Celebrating the Baby Bump*. Stanford, CA: Stanford University Press, Stanford Law, Cultural Lives of Law series.

Cramer, Renee Ann (2012) 'The Baby Bump Is the New Birkin', in Shira Tarrant & Marjorie Jolles, eds. *Fashion Talks: Undressing the Power of Style*. Albany, NY: SUNY Press, 53–66.

Crawford, Patricia & Sara Mendelson (1998) *Women in Early Modern England*. Oxford: Clarendon Press.

Croyden, Margaret (2003) *Conversations with Peter Brook 1970–2000*. London: Faber and Faber.

Darlington, W. A. (1960) *Six Thousand and One Nights: 40 Years a Critic*. London: George G. Harrup.

Davidson, Hilary (2023) *Jane Austen's Wardrobe*. New Haven: Yale University Press.

de Marly, Diana (1982) *Costumes on the Stage 1600–1940*. London: B.T. Batsford.

Dench, Judi, with Brendan O'Hea (2023) *Shakespeare: The Man Who Pays the Rent*. London: Michael Joseph.

Dench, Judi (2010) *And Furthermore: As Told to John Miller*. London: Weidenfeld & Nicholson.

Dobson, Michael (2010) 'John Philip Kemble', in *Great Shakespeareans: Garrick, Kemble, Siddons, Keen*. Peter Holland, ed. London: Continuum, 55–104.

Dobson, Michael (2001) 'On the Page and on the Stage', in Margreta de Grazia & Stanley Wells, eds. *The Cambridge Companion to Shakespeare*. Cambridge: Cambridge University Press, 235–50.

Doran, Gregory (2023) *My Shakespeare: A Director's Journey through the First Folio*. London: Methuen.

Dunbar, Mary Judith (2010) *Shakespeare in Performance: The Winter's Tale*. With a chapter by Carol Chillington Rutter. Manchester: Manchester University Press.

Dunworth, Felicity (2010) *Mothers and Meanings on the Early Modern English Stage*. Manchester: Manchester University Press.

Dymkowski, Christine (1986) *Harley Granville Barker: A Preface to Modern Shakespeare*. Washington, DC: Folger Books.

Edelstein, T. J. (1994) *The Stage Is All the World: The Theatrical Designs of Tanya Moiseiwitsch*. Chicago, IL: The David and Alfred Smart Museum, University of Chicago.

Engel, Laura (2024) *The Art of the Actress: Fashioning Identities*. Cambridge Elements. Cambridge: Cambridge University Press.

Ephraim, Michelle (2016) 'Hermione's Suspicious Body: Adultery and Superfetation in *The Winter's Tale*', in Kathryn M. Moncrief & Kathryn R. McPherson, eds. *Performing Maternity in Early Modern England*, Surrey: Ashgate, 2007, rpt. Routledge Studies in Performance and Early Modern Drama. Routledge, 2016, 45–58.

Escolme, Bridget (2020) *Shakespeare and Costume in Practice*. Cham: Palgrave Macmillan.

Evans, Gareth Lloyd (1970) 'Interpretation or Experiment?', in Kenneth Muir, ed. *Shakespeare Survey 23*. Cambridge: Cambridge University Press, 131–35, (132).

Faucit, Helena, Lady Martin (1891) *Shakespeare's Female Characters*. London: Blackwood & Sons.

Filippini, Maria Nadia (2021) *Pregnancy, Delivery, Childbirth*, Clelia Boscolo, trans. London: Routledge.

Foakes, R. A. (1961) *Henslowe's Diary*. Cambridge: Cambridge University Press, 2nd ed. 2002.

Gilbreath, Alexandra (2003) 'Hermione in *The Winter's Tale*', in Robert Smallwood, ed. *Players of Shakespeare 5*. Cambridge: University of Cambridge Press, 74–90.

Granville-Barker, Harley (1912), 'Preface', in *The Winter's Tale: An Acting Edition* William Heinemann, iii–x, reprinted in *Prefaces to Shakespeare*. vol VI. London: B.T. Batsford, 1974, 19–25.

Griffin, Alice (1963) The New York Shakespeare Festival 1963. *Shakespeare Quarterly* vol. xiv. New York: The Shakespeare Association of America, 441–43.

Gurr, Andrew (2009) *The Shakespearean Stage 1574–1642*. Cambridge: Cambridge University Press, 4th ed.

Hall, Edward & Roger Warren (2012) *Propeller Shakespeare: The Winter's Tale*. London: Oberon Books.

Hardwick, J. M. D. (1954) *Emigrant in Motley: The Journey of Charles and Ellen Kean in Quest of a Theatrical Fortune in Australia and America, as Told in Their Hitherto Unpublished Letters*. Forward by Anthony Quayle. London: Rockliff.

Hawkins, Ella (2022) *Shakespeare in Elizabethan Costume: 'Period Dress' In Twenty-First-Century Performance*. The Arden Shakespeare. London: Bloomsbury.

Hearn, Karen (2020) *Portraying Pregnancy: from Holbein to Social Media*. London: Paul Holberton Publishing in Association with the Foundling Museum.

Hearn, Karen (1995) *Dynasties: Painting in Tudor and Jacobean England 1530–1630*. Peterborough: Tate Gallery.

Henslowe, Philip (1961) *Henslowe's Diary*. ed. R. A. Folkes, Cambridge: Cambridge University Press, 2nd ed. 2002.

Hicks, Greg (2010) Interview in *Lectures de The winter's tale de William Shakespeare*. Delphine Lemonnier-Texier & Guillaume Winter, eds. Rennes: Presses Universitaires de Rennes.

Hobby, Elaine (2009) 'Introduction', in *The Birth of Mankind: Otherwise Named, The Woman's Book*. Literary and Scientific Culture in Early Modernity series, Surrey: Ashgate.

Hodgdon, Barbara (2016) *Shakespeare, Performance and the Archive*. London: Routledge.

Hodgdon, Barbara (2006) 'Shopping in the archives: material memories' in Peter Holland, ed. *Shakespeare, Memory and Performance*. Cambridge: Cambridge University Press, 135–67.

Holland, Peter (2001) 'Shakespeare in the twentieth century', in *The Cambridge Companion to Shakespeare*. *Cambridge*: Cambridge University Press 199–216.

Holt, Annie (2021) *Modernizing Costume Design, 1820–1920*. London: Routledge.

Hunter, Kelly (2015) *Cracking Shakespeare: A Hands-on Guide for Actors and Directors + Video*. London: Bloomsbury.

Hutchings, Geoffrey (1989) 'Lavatch in *All's Well That Ends Well*' in *Players of Shakespeare*. Philip Brockbank, ed. Cambridge, Cambridge University Press. pp.77–90.

Isaac, Veronica (2021) '"Re-Dressing the Part": The Scenographic Strategies of Ellen Terry (1847–1928),' *Scenography and Art History: Performance*

Design and Visual Culture. Astrid von Rosen & Viveka Kjellmer, eds. London: Bloomsbury Visual Arts, 2021.

Isaac, Veronica (2020) 'Costume Centre Stage: Re-membering Ellen Terry', in Sofia Pantouvaki & Peter McNeil, eds. *Performance Costume: New Perspectives*. London: Bloomsbury, 69–88.

Isaac, Veronica (2018) '"A Well-Dressed Actress": Exploring the Theatrical Wardrobe of Ellen Terry (1847–1928)', *Costume* 52.1, 74–96.

Jackson, Russell (2019) *Shakespeare in the Theatre: Trevor Nunn*. The Arden Shakespeare. London: Bloomsbury.

Jackson, Russell (2015) 'Brief Overview: A Stage History of Shakespeare and Costume', in Patricia Lennox & Bella Mirabella, eds. *Shakespeare and Costume*. The Arden Shakespeare. London: Bloomsbury, 10–20.

Jansted, Janelle (2016) 'Smock-Secrets: Birth and Women's Mysteries on the Early Modern Stage', in Kathryn M. Moncrief & Kathryn R. McPherson, eds. *Performing Maternity in Early Modern England*. Surrey: Ashgate, 2007, reprinted in Routledge Studies in Performance and Early Modern Drama. London: Routledge 2016, 87–100.

Jones, Ann Rosalind & Peter Stallybrass (2000) *Renaissance Clothing and the Material of Memory*. Cambridge: Cambridge University Press.

Jones, Gemma (1989) 'Hermione in *The Winter's Tale*', in Philip Brockbank, ed. *Players of Shakespeare 1*. Cambridge: Cambridge University Press, 153–65.

Kavanagh, Julie (1996) *Secret Muses: The Life of Frederick Ashton*. London: Faber & Faber.

Kean, Charles (1856) *The Winter's Tale: Charles Kean 1856*. Facsimile, London: Cornmarket Press.

Kellermann, Jonas (2021) '"Like an Old Tale": *The Winter's Tale* on the Balletic Stage', in *Shakespeare Jahrbuch*. 157/2021, 162–79.

Kemble, John Philip. *The Winter's Tale: John Philip Kemble Promptbooks*. vol 9, Charles H. Shattuck, ed. Charlottesville: University Press of Virginia.

Kennard, Nina H. (Mrs A.) (1893) *Mrs Siddons*. London: W. H. Allen.

Kennedy, Dennis (1985) *Granville Barker and the Dream of Theatre*. Cambridge: Cambridge University Press.

Kirwan, Peter (2022). 'Shakespeare Performances in England, 2021: Productions Outside London' in Emma Smith, ed. *Shakespeare Survey 75*. Cambridge: Cambridge University Press. 342–56.

Klett, Elizabeth (2020) *Choreographing Shakespeare: Dance Adaptations of the Plays and Poems*. London: Routledge.

Kustow, Michael (2005) *Peter Brook: A Biography*. London: Bloomsbury.

Laoutaris, Chris (2008) *Shakespearean Maternities: Crisis of Conception in Early Modern England*. Edinburgh: Edinburgh University Press.

Laver, James (1964) *Costume in the Theatre*. London: George G. Harrap.

Lee, Mireille (2005) 'Constru(ct)ing Gender in the Feminine Greek Peplos', in Liza Cleland, Mary Harlow, & Lloyd Llewellyn-Jones, eds. *The Clothed Body in the Ancient World*. Oxford: Oxbow Books.

Lennox, Patricia (2015) 'How Designers Helped Juliet's Nurse Reclaim Her Bawdy', in Patricia Lennox & Bella Mirabella, eds. *Shakespeare and Costume*. The Arden Shakespeare. London: Bloomsbury, 157–84.

Lennox, Patricia (2022) *The Comedy of Errors* Review, *Shakespeare Bulletin*, vol 4, no. 2, 275–9.

Luckyj, Christina (2007) 'Disciplining the Mother in Seventeenth-Century English Puritanism', in Kathryn M. Moncrief & Kathryn R. McPherson, eds. *Performing Maternity in Early Modern England*. Surrey: Ashgate, 2007, Routledge Studies in Performance and Early Modern Drama. London: Routledge, 2016, 101–14.

MacIntyre, Jean (1992) *Costumes and Scripts in the Elizabethan Theatres*. Alberta: University of Alberta.

Marshall, Gail (1998) *Actresses on the Victorian Stage*. Cambridge: Cambridge University Press.

Martin, Theodore, Sir (1900) *Helena Faucit (Lady Martin)*. London: William Blackwood and Sons.

McCarthy, Harry M. (2022) *Boy Actors in Early Modern England*. Cambridge: Cambridge University Press.

McCarthy, Harry M. (2020) *Performing Early Modern Drama beyond Shakespeare: Edward's Boys*. Elements in Shakespeare Performance. Cambridge: Cambridge University Press.

McCarthy, Lillah O. B. E. (Lady Keeble) (1933) *Myself and My Friends*. London: Thornton Butterworth.

Miller, Gina (2020) *Childhood in Contemporary Performance of Shakespeare*. The Arden Shakespeare. London: Bloomsbury.

Moncrief, Kathryn M. & Kathryn R. McPherson eds. (2007) *Performing Maternity in Early Modern England*. Surrey: Ashgate, 2007, Routledge Studies in Performance and Early Modern Drama. London: Routledge 2016.

Monks, Aoife (2020) *The Actor in Costume*. Basingstoke: Palgrave McMillan.

Nussbaum, Felicity (2010) *Rival Queens: Actresses. Performance, and the Eighteenth-Century British Theatre*. Philadelphia: University of Pennsylvania Press.

Odell, George C. D. (1966) *Shakespeare from Betterton to Irving*. 2 vols. New York: Dover.

Pavelka, Michael (2012) 'Designing *the Winter's Tale*', in Edward Hall & Roger Warren, eds. *Propeller Shakespeare: The Winter's Tale*. London: Oberon Books,14–16.

Phillips, Chelsea (2022) *Carrying All before Her: Celebrity Pregnancy 1689–1800*. Newark: University of Delaware Press.

Poiret, Paul (1931), Stephen Haden Guest, trans. (2009). *King of Fashion: The Autobiography of Paul Poiret*. J.B. Lippincott; reprint, London: V&A, 2009.

Potter, Lois (2014) 'A Sacred Trust: Helen Faucit, Geraldine Jewsbury, and the Idealized Shakespeare', in *Shakespeare Theatre and Effects of Performance*,

Farah Karim Cooper & Tiffany Stern, eds. Arden Shakespeare. London: Bloomsbury. 183–99.

Potter, Lois (2001) 'Shakespeare in the Theatre 1660–1900', in Margreta de Grazia and Stanley Wells, eds. *The Cambridge Companion to Shakespeare*. Cambridge: Cambridge University Press, 183–99.

Purcell, Stephen (2018) 'Shakespeare Performances in England, 2017', in Peter Holland, ed., *Shakespeare Survey 71*, 2018. Cambridge: Cambridge University Press, 305–8.

Ribeiro, Aileen (2003) 'Costuming the Part: A Discourse of Fashion and Fiction in the Image of the Actress in England, 1776–1812', in Robyn Asleson, ed. *Notorious Muse: The Actress in British Art and Culture 1776–1812*. New Haven, CT: Yale University Press, 104–28.

Ribeyrol, Charlotte, Matthew Winterbottom, & Madeline Hewitson, eds. (2024) *Colour Revolution: Victorian Art, Fashion & Design*. Oxford: Ashmolean Museum, Oxford University.

Ritchie, Fiona (2023) *Shakespeare in the Theatre: Sarah Siddons and John Philip Kemble*. The Arden Shakespeare. London: Bloomsbury.

Roberts, Jeanne (1992) 'Shakespeare's Maimed Birth Rites', in Linda Woodbridge & Edward Berry, eds. *True Rites and Maimed Rites: Ritual and Anti-ritual in Shakespeare and His Age*. Urbana: University of Illinois Press, 123–44.

Rokison-Woodall, Abigail (2017) *Shakespeare in the Theatre: Nicholas Hytner*. The Arden Shakespeare. London: Bloomsbury.

Rothfeld, Becca (2024) *All Things Are Too Small: Essays in Praise of Excess* New York: Henry Holt.

Rutter, Carol Chillington (2010) "A World Ransomed, or One Destroyed": English *Tales* at the Millennium', in Judith Dunbar, ed. *Shakespeare in Performance: The Winter's Tale*. Shakespeare in Performance. Manchester: Manchester University. 213–42.

Rutter, Carol Chillington (2007) *Shakespeare and Child's Play*. London: Routledge.

Rutter, Carol Chillington (1988) *Clamorous Voices: Shakespeare's Women Today*. London: The Women's Press.

Sacks, Elizabeth (1980) *Shakespeare's Images of Pregnancy*. London: Macmillan.

Scheijen, Sjeng (2010) *Diaghilev: A Life*. London: Profile Press.

Scholz, Susanne (2000) *Body Narratives: Writing the Nation and Fashioning the Subject in Early Modern England*. New York: St. Martin's Press.

Shakespeare, William (2020) *Measure for Measure*, A. R. Braunmuller, ed. The Arden Shakespeare. London: Bloomsbury. Reprint 2024.

Shakespeare, William (2017) *A Midsummer Night's Dream*, Shukanta Chaudhuri, ed. The Arden Shakespeare. London: Bloomsbury.

Shakespeare, William (2017) *The Comedy of Errors*. Ken Cartwright, ed. The Arden Shakespeare. London: Bloomsbury.

Shakespeare, William (2016) *King Henry 4* part 2, James C. Bulman, ed. The Arden Shakespeare. London: Bloomsbury.

Shakespeare, William (2012) *Propeller Shakespeare: The Winter's Tale*. Edward Hall & Roger Warren, eds. London: Oberon Books.

Shakespeare, William (2010) *The Winter's Tale*, John Pitcher, ed. The Arden Shakespeare. London: Bloomsbury. Reprint 2014.

Shakespeare, William (1998) *Love's Labour's Lost*, H. R. Woudhuysen, ed. The Arden Shakespeare. London: Bloomsbury.

Shakespeare, William & Fletcher, John (2000) *King Henry VIII (All Is True)*, Gordon McMullan, ed. The Arden Shakespeare. London: Bloomsbury.

Shattuck, Charles H. ed. (1974) *John Philip Kemble Promptbooks*. vol 9. The Folger Facsimile Promptbooks, Series I. Charlottesville: Published for the Folger Shakespeare Library by the University Press of Virginia.

Shaughnessy, Richard (2020) *About Shakespeare: Bodies, Spaces and Texts.* Elements in Shakespeare Performance. Cambridge: Cambridge University Press.

Shaw, George Bernard (1933) 'An Aside', in Lillah McCarthy, *Myself and My Friends*. London: Thornton Butterworth, 1–8.

Sher, Antony (2003) 'Leontes in *The Winter's Tale* and *Macbeth*', in *Players of Shakespeare 5*. Robert Smallwood, ed. Cambridge: Cambridge University Press, 91–112.

Shrimpton, Nicholas (1987) 'Shakespeare Performances in London, Manchester and Stratford upon Avon 1985–86', in *Shakespeare Survey 40*, Stanley Wells, ed. Cambridge: Cambridge University Press, 177–78.

Siddons, Sarah Kemble (1942) *The Reminiscences of Sarah Kemble Siddons 1773–1785*, William ban Lennep, ed. Cambridge, MA: Printed at Widener Library.

Sprague, Arthur Colby (1948) *Shakespeare and the Actors: The Stage Business in His Plays 1660–1905.* 4th printing. Cambridge, MA: Harvard University Press.

Stage Year Book 1914. Covent Garden, London: The Stage Offices.

Stedman, Jane W. (1996) *W.S. Gilbert: A Classic Victorian and His Theatre*. Oxford: Oxford University Press.

Stewart, Patrick (2023) *Making It So: A Memoir*. London: Gallery Books UK.

Styan, J. L. (1977) *The Shakespeare Revolution*. Cambridge: Cambridge University Press.

Styan, J. L. (1984) *Shakespeare in Performance: All's Well that Ends Well*. Manchester: Manchester University Press.

Tatspaugh, Patricia E. (2002) *Shakespeare at Stratford: The Winter's Tale*. London: The Arden Shakespeare in association with the Shakespeare Birthplace Trust.

Terry, Ellen (1932) *Ellen Terry's Memoirs*, Edith Craig & Christopher St. John, eds. New York: G.P. Putnam's Sons.

Terry, Ellen (1908) *The Story of My Life*. London: Hutchinson.

Theatre World Annual 1952, vol 3, 1951–1952. Frances Stephens, ed. London: Rockliffe, 36–40.

Thiel, S. B. T. (2018) '"Cushion Come Forth": Materializing Pregnancy on the Stuart Stage', in Annalisa Castaldo & Rhonda Knight, eds. *Stage Matters: Props, Bodies, and Space in Shakespeare Performance*. Madison, NJ: Farleigh Dickinson University Press, 143–58.

Trewin, J. C., ed. (1967) *The Journal of William Charles Macready, 1832–1851*. London: Longmans.

Trewin, J. C. (1971) *Peter Brook: A Biography*. London: Macdonald.

Walter, Harriet (2016) *Brutus and Other Heroines: Playing Shakespeare's Roles for Women*. London: Nick Hearn Books.

Warren, Roger (1988) 'Shakespeare's Late Plays at Stratford Ontario 1985–86', in Stanley Wells, ed., *Shakespeare Survey 40*. Cambridge: Cambridge University Press, 155–68.

Wells, Stanley (1989) 'Shakespeare Performances in England 1987–88', in Stanley Wells, ed., *Shakespeare Survey 39*. Cambridge: Cambridge University Press, 193–97.

Acknowledgements

The Winter's Tale is well served by three excellent books on its performance history: Dennis Bartholomeusz (1982) on England and America 1611 to 1976, Patricia E. Tatspaugh (2002) on RSC and other Stratford-upon-Avon productions from 1948 to 1986, and Judith Dunbar (2010) on selected international performances 1912 to 1997, which includes Carol Chillington Rutter's chapter, 'English *Tales* at the millennium'. *Performing Visible Pregnancy in Shakespeare's Plays* began as a conference paper for '"Strange Habits"' / Strange Habitats' organized by Sophie Chiari and Anne-Marie Miller-Blaise, May 2020, Clermont-Ferrand, France (cancelled by covid). The Royal Shakespeare Company (RSC) performance archives provided much of the twentieth- and twenty-first-century material. These are stored in the Shakespeare Birthplace Trust Collection (SBT) in Stratford-upon-Avon, where the librarians and curators have been consistently helpful and resourceful, even when working under constricted post-covid conditions. The Shakespeare Institute of the University of Birmingham has been a major source of primary and secondary printed material. Its librarians, especially Kate Welch, have been unfailingly welcoming, helpful, and supportive. Sourcing high-resolution photographs was made possible through the help of curators at Harvard University's Houghton Library, the RSC, and the SBT Collection photo team, particularly Andrew Thomas. So many people have shared their own knowledge and experience, and they have my deepest gratitude. These include: Patricia E. Tatspaugh for encouragement, her RSC performance history and for introducing me to Sarah Siddons' statue in Paddington Green; Miriam Gilbert for listening, advising, recommending, and generosity. Maria Meale shared her experiences as part of the RSC 1986 production; Dominique Goy-Blanquet provided information on French productions; Veronica Isaac shared information from her deep research on Ellen Terry; and Judi Dench set the record straight on Nunn. Most especially there is Russell Jackson who shares his research notes and life with me.

Cambridge Elements

Shakespeare Performance

W. B. Worthen
Barnard College

W. B. Worthen is Alice Brady Pels Professor in the Arts, and Chair of the Theatre Department at Barnard College. He is also co-chair of the Ph.D. Program in Theatre at Columbia University, where he is Professor of English and Comparative Literature.

ADVISORY BOARD

Pascale Aebischer, University of Exeter
Todd Landon Barnes, Ramapo College of New Jersey
Susan Bennett, University of Calgary
Rustom Bharucha, Jawaharlal Nehru University, New Delhi
Gina Bloom, University of California, Davis
Bridget Escolme, Queen Mary University of London
Alan Galey, University of Toronto
Douglas Lanier, University of New Hampshire
Julia Reinhard Lupton, University of California, Irvine
Peter W. Marx, University of Köln
Sonia Massai, King's College London
Alfredo Michel Modenessi, National Autonomous University of Mexico
Robert Shaughnessy, Guildford School of Acting, University of Surrey
Ayanna Thompson, George Washington University
Yong Li-Lan, National University of Singapore

ABOUT THE SERIES
Shakespeare Performance is a dynamic collection in a field that is both always emerging and always evanescent. Responding to the global range of Shakespeare performance today, the series launches provocative, urgent criticism for researchers, graduate students and practitioners. Publishing scholarship with a direct bearing on the contemporary contexts of Shakespeare performance, it considers specific performances, material and social practices, ideological and cultural frameworks, emerging and significant artists and performance histories.

Cambridge Elements

Shakespeare Performance

ELEMENTS IN THE SERIES

This Distracted Globe: Attending to Distraction in Shakespeare's Theatre
Jennifer J. Edwards

Shakespeare without Print
Paul Menzer

Shakespeare's Visionary Women
Laura Jayne Wright

Early Modern Media Ecology
Peter W. Marx

Sleep No More and the Discourses of Shakespeare Performance
D. J. Hopkins

Staging Disgust: Rape, Shame, and Performance in Shakespeare and Middleton
Jennifer Panek

Extended Reality Shakespeare
Aneta Mancewicz

Approaching the Interval in the Early Modern Theatre: The Significance of the 'Act-Time'
Mark Hutchings

Shakespeare and Nonhuman Intelligence
Heather Warren-Crow

Shakespeare and the Restoration Repertory
Stephen Watkins

Performing Shakespeare on an Endangered Planet
Katherine Brokaw and Elizabeth Freestone

Performing Visible Pregnancy in Shakespeare's Plays
Patricia Lennox

A full series listing is available at: www.cambridge.org/ESPF

For EU product safety concerns, contact us at Calle de José Abascal, 56–1°,
28003 Madrid, Spain or eugpsr@cambridge.org.

www.ingramcontent.com/pod-product-compliance
Lightning Source LLC
LaVergne TN
LVHW011845060526
838200LV00054B/4179